Ethics Year 2

A Level Revision Guide

OCR H573/2

2016 Specification

Peter Baron

Published by Active Education

www.peped.org

First published in 2017

ISBN: 978-1979549905

Cartoons used with permission © Becky Dyer

All images © their respective owners

Links, reviews, news and revision materials available on

www.peped.org

www.peped.org website allows students and teachers to explore Philosophy of Religion and Ethics through handouts, film clips, presentations, case studies, extracts, games and academic articles.

Pitched just right, and so much more than a text book, here is a place to engage with critical reflection whatever your level. Marked student essays are also posted.

Contents

'The unexamined life is not worth living' Socrates

About this Guide

The OCR 2016 specification H573 has posed unique challenges for teacher and student, and for this reason I am developing a new approach to revision which integrates elements of the peped project.

- The textbooks have produced their own interpretation of the specification which you don't necessarily need to follow. They have overlaid an additional discussion of philosophers and philosophical ideas in order to evaluate the fairly brief content of the specification. So it is essential you understand that you will be examined on knowledge and content alone - and you can use whoever you like to evaluate and criticise this content. You will notice that, for example, **BUTLER** and **NEWMAN** remain in this guide (under Section 5, Conscience) even though only Freud and Aquinas are named in the specification, because you need to bounce some philosophers off the named ones. **You should download and print out now a hard copy of the relevant pages of the specification**.

- The three papers need to be integrated to produce what is called **SYNOPTIC** insight. This literally means elements of the three papers that can be 'seen together' or linked up. For example, Kant's **MORAL ARGUMENT** (Philosophy of Religion) links and to his ethics which links to **HICK**'s universal **PLURALISM** (Christian Thought) as Hick is greatly inspired by Kant. I have done a lot of work on the peped website showing how to integrate the three papers and there will be a **REVISION** section accessible for those who have this guide showing you how to increase your synoptic understanding. **Those who have this guide should have a head-start, but you need to supplement it with my other ideas and sample answers.**

- Our approach is to teach for **STRUCTURES OF THOUGHT**. These are given by the mindmaps in this guide. Notice these are not free-for-all scatter diagrams but are structures that move form worldview through to conclusion. And the same structure will be there in the website and in the other revision materials I am writing - with creative and hopefully fun tasks you can use to test your understanding. **You need to run with this concept which I believe makes our approach unique, and if you do so, your chances of an A grade or A* will be greatly enhanced.**

Peped represents a community of teachers who are talking and testing things all the time, in a great co-operative conversation.

We are talking with two aims in mind: to put the 'wow!' back into Religious Studies and make sure hard concepts are made crystal clear and then applied through everyday culture.

Yes, even Augustine's doctrine of original sin or Kant's categorical imperative have echoes in our culture today.

And ultimately we'll only be good philosophers and A* candidates if we have learned to read our culture and make sure our answers are full of relevance as well as crystal clarity and razor-sharp evaluation.

For peped Revision events please go to the website and look under 'events', and you can meet us in person!

Introduction to Ethics

In Year 1 (specification sections 1-3) we introduced **DEONTOLOGICAL** and **TELEOLOGICAL** ethics and asked the question: to what extent is ethics **ABSOLUTE** or **RELATIVE**? We then applied the **NORMATIVE** ethical theories of Situation Ethics and Natural Law to euthanasia, and Kantian Ethics and Utilitarianism to business ethics.

In Year 2 sections 4-6 of the specification, the theories are now retained and a number of new issues considered in the nature and origin of **CONSCIENCE** (section 5). To deontology and teleology we add a study of the foundation of ethics - **META-ETHICS** (section 4), which includes the study of ethical meaning of the word "good' or "bad".

SEXUAL ETHICS (Section 6) is added as an applied issue (homosexuality, sex before marriage, and adultery). The specification asks us to consider,

"How the study of ethics has, over time, influenced and been influenced by developments in religious beliefs and practices, societal norms and normative theories". OCR H573 Specification

Both our **DEONTOLOGICAL THEORIES** (Kant and Natural Law - though Natural Law isn't pure deontology as it has a teleological aspect in the rational goals we pursue as human beings) and our **TELEOLOGICAL THEORIES** (Utilitarianism and Situation Ethics) are applied to issues surrounding **SEXUAL ETHICS**. Notice the following requirements to understand:

- traditional religious beliefs and practices (from any religious perspectives) regarding these areas of sexual ethics - for example as formed in Catholic **NATURAL LAW** theory and Papal Encyclicals (circulated letters) such as Humanae Vitae (1968)

- how these beliefs and practices have changed over time, including:

  o key teachings influencing these beliefs and practices

  o the ideas of religious figures and institutions

- the impact of **SECULARISM** (see also Christian Thought, paper 3, section 5) on these areas of sexual ethics

Notice that the work of **SIGMUND FREUD** on the unconscious and the **OEDIPUS COMPLEX** may also be relevant here (see section on Conscience). Together with **RICHARD DAWKINS** these are figures in our syllabus who form a basis for considering a secular worldview.

KEY TERMS

- **META-ETHICS** - concerns the nature and meaning of the words good and right. A key question in meta-ethics is: "Is goodness **OBJECTIVE** (linked to moral facts in the world) or **SUBJECTIVE** (up to me)?"

- **CONSCIENCE** - may come from **GOD**, our **UPBRINGING** or a process of **REASON**. "Where does conscience come from and how does it operate?" **PSYCHOLOGY** merges with philosophy here.

- **INTRINSIC THEORIES OF VALUE** - see something as good-in-itself. Does the pleasure for example have intrinsic value?

- **INSTRUMENTAL THEORIES OF VALUE** - see goodness relative to some end, such as human happiness. But in the debates within ethics, what do **DEONTOLOGISTS** like Kant or **TELEOLOGISTS** like Joseph Fletcher or JS Mill have to say about sexual ethics?

THE ETHICS TOOLKIT

The study of ethical theories so far has equipped us with a toolkit which we can use to assess any ethical issue. In this toolkit we derive insights from different theories.

KANT has given us the **PRINCIPLE OF UNIVERSALISABILITY**, a method of reasoning implying **CONSISTENCY** and a neutral point of view, and **PERSONAL AUTONOMY**, that places human choice and reason as a central ethical concern.

AQUINAS has given us the **PRINCIPLE OF NATURAL RATIONAL PURPOSE:** the idea of an order of being which is appropriate to our unique rational natures. The ultimate **TELOS** is **EUDAIMONIA** – well-being or personal and social flourishing.

UTILITARIANS have given us the **GREATEST HAPPINESS PRINCIPLE** and the **LEAST HARM PRINCIPLE**: the idea that we should always assess consequences in the light of an empirical calculation of the balance of happiness over misery, pleasure over pain or **WELFARE** over harm. In Economics we talk of **COST/BENEFIT** analysis.

RELATIVISTS encourage us to consider the **PRINCIPLE OF CULTURAL DIVERSITY** and to be humble in the face of claims that our own culture is objectively superior. All theories are to some extent children of their times.

It is important to note that our theories overlap to some extent and may not be as opposed as we sometimes think. For example, all of them discuss and claim for themselves the **GOLDEN RULE** "Do to others as you would have them do to you", Matthew 7:18 (is this therefore a good example of a universal ethical **ABSOLUTE**?).

All appeal to **VIRTUE** or character traits (**MILL** appeals to sympathy, **KANT** to dutifulness, **FLETCHER** to love, **AQUINAS** to practical wisdom and the Christian virtues of I Corinthians 13, faith, hope and love).

All theories have a **TELEOLOGICAL** aspect. Kant for example considers consequences in so far as he asks us to universalise the consequences of everyone doing what I do. He also envisages a goal, the **SUMMUM BONUM** which is similar in some ways to Aristotle's **EUDAIMONIA**. Moreover, Aquinas' **NATURAL LAW** is best described as "a deontological theory arising out of a Greek teleological worldview" where the good is defined by the rational end (**TELOS**).

Meta-Ethics

ISSUES

META-ETHICS means "beyond ethics" (metaphysics - beyond physics). Rather than asking how we derive moral principles like "do not kill", meta-ethics asks us to consider what moral statements mean and what the **FOUNDATION** of ethics might be. Here are some of the key issues:

Is there an **OBJECTIVE** principle we can appeal to resolve moral disputes? Or are we inevitably in a world of **RELATIVISM** and **SUBJECTIVISM** where such questions are "up to me"?

When I say "stealing is wrong" am I describing some **FACTS** about the world which we can look at, examine, appeal to, or am I only stating an opinion or expressing a feeling?

Is moral **LANGUAGE** a special type of language where words like "good" and "ought" mean something quite specific and different from other uses of, for example, "good"? Is the meaning of good in the sentence "that's a good painting" different from the moral use "good boy!"?

SPECIFICATION

NATURALISM (the belief that values can be defined in terms of some natural property in the world) and its application to **ABSOLUTISM**

INTUITIONISM (the belief that basic moral truths are indefinable but self-evident) and its application to the term good

EMOTIVISM (the belief that ethical terms evince approval or disapproval) and its application to **RELATIVISM**

KEY TERMS

- **ANALYTIC** - true by definition "all bachelors are unmarried".

- **SYNTHETIC** - true by observation "John is a bachelor".

- **A PRIORI** - before experience.

- **A POSTERIORI** - after experience.

- **COGNITIVISM** - moral facts can be known objectively as **TRUE** or **FALSE**.

- **NATURALISM** - moral goodness is a feature of the natural world, and so an **A POSTERIORI** fact.

- **NATURALISTIC FALLACY** - you cannot move without supplying a missing **PREMISE** from a descriptive statement such as "kindness causes pleasure" to a moral statement "kindness is good".

Note: Hume was himself a the father of the utilitarian naturalists as he argued that morality derives from the natural feeling of sympathy. He never said "you cannot move from an ought to an is", but only that if we do so, we must provide a missing premise with a value-statement in it, such as "pleasure is good as it leads to a happy life". However Hume's theory of language is developed by **AJ AYER** in the theory of **EMOTIVISM** - a non-naturalist theory of how moral language works and Hume never supplied the missing premise himself (but implies that the origin of morality is found in naturalistic sentiments of approval).

STRUCTURE OF THOUGHT

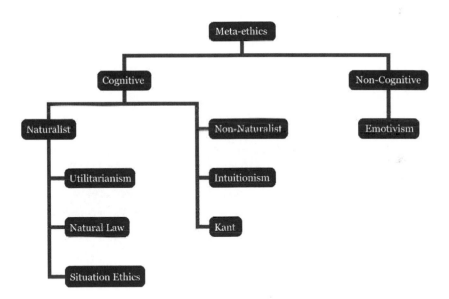

COGNITIVE or NON-COGNITIVE

COGNITIVISTS believe goodness can be known as an **OBJECTIVE** feature of the world - where "objective" means "out there where it can be analysed, measured, and assessed". So cognitivism says "ethical statements can be proved true or false".

Something about our reason allows us to do this either by making some measurement (for example of happiness as the utilitarians do) or working out a principle **A PRIORI**, before experience, as Kant argues we do in deriving the **CATEGORICAL IMPERATIVE**.

NON-COGNITIVISTS argue there is no objective, factual basis for morality - it is subjective and up to me to determine. Ethical statements don't have **TRUTH VALUE** - they are empirically unprovable. Put another way - **NON-COGNITIVISTS** can say 'there is no such thing as a moral fact" such as the fact of pleasure or pain identified by Utilitarians.

The **NATURALISTS** argue we can resolve this issue empirically (**A POSTERIORI** - from experience) by looking at some observable feature of an action - a fact such as "it causes pain" (a utilitarian concern) or "it fulfils the natural rational purpose of human beings" (the **EUDAIMONIA** or goal of flourishing of **NATURAL LAW**).

NON-NATURALISTS argue either that the truth is a priori (Kant for example, even though he argues for **COGNITIVISM**) or that there are simply no facts which we can identify as moral facts – so that making a moral statement adds nothing to what we already know from a factual basis. This form of **NON-COGNITIVIST** non-naturalism is called **EMOTIVISM**.

THE NATURALISTIC FALLACY

Developing a point made by David Hume, philosophers like **GE MOORE** have argued that when we move from a description about the real world to a moral statement we make a leap from a naturalistic statement to a **PRESCRIPTIVE** statement (one with ought in it). This prescription is doing something different. What we often fail to do is explain the missing link between a description and a prescription - and this leap from is to ought is what is known as the **NATURALISTIC FALLACY**. A.N. Prior (1949) explains the fallacy:

> *"Because some quality or combination of qualities invariably accompanies the quality of goodness, this quality or combination of qualities is identical with goodness. If, for example, it is believed that whatever is pleasant is good, or that whatever is good must be pleasant, or both, it is committing the naturalistic fallacy to infer from this that goodness and pleasantness are the same quality. The naturalistic fallacy is the assumption that because the words 'good' and 'pleasant' necessarily describe the same objects, they must attribute the same quality to them".*

MOORE argued that goodness cannot be a **COMPLEX** analysable property of an action. For example a horse can be broken down into animal, mammal, four legs, hairy tail – a **COMPLEX** idea. Because goodness isn't a complex idea, it must be either a **SIMPLE**, indefinable quality or it doesn't refer to anything at all. Since ethics isn't an **ILLUSION**, goodness must consist in a simple **INDEFINABLE QUALITY**, like the colour yellow.

THE OPEN QUESTION

Moore pointed out that the naturalistic fallacy, of implying that goodness was identical to some specific property such as pleasure, is susceptible to the **OPEN QUESTION** attack. Suppose I say "this ice cream causes me so much pleasure" and then say "ice cream is good!". The open question attack suggests I can always ask the question "it produces pleasure, but nonetheless, is it morally **GOOD**?"

If I can answer "no" to this point then I have proved that goodness is something independent of pleasure.

MOORE's INTUITIONISM

Moore was a non-naturalist **COGNITIVIST** because he believed that goodness could not be defined by its natural properties, but that we know what we mean by good by a special intuition or perception (so **COGNITIVIST**, as goodness can be known as a shared experience).

Moore argues goodness is an **INDEFINABLE PROPERTY** of an action just as the colour yellow is a non-definable property of a lemon - we know what it is and that's the end of it. We can try and reduce yellowness to light waves but that doesn't precisely tell us what yellow is - yellow just is yellow, we know this by intuition. Notice this is a version of non-naturalism as goodness cannot be established as a fact of sense experience, but as a **NON-NATURALISTIC** perception.

EVALUATION OF INTUITIONISM

Moral intuitions are said to be like the **ANALYTIC** truths of Mathematics. But moral statements are more than just "true by definition". Peter Singer comments:

"Thus the intuitionists lost the one useful analogy to support the existence of a body of truths known by reason alone".

Intuitionists **CAN'T AGREE** what these moral goods are. So how can they be **SELF-EVIDENT**? Moreover, Moore's theory is also open to his own **OPEN QUESTION** attack on ethical **NATURALISM**: "that may be your intuition (eg genocide is okay), but is it **GOOD**?"

If intuitions are actually **CULTURAL CONSTRUCTS** as Freud suggests, then they cannot be **SELF-EVIDENT**.

Moore is arguing that moral truths are similar to **PLATO**'s ideal forms. John Maynard **KEYNES** once commented that "Moore could not distinguish love, and beauty and truth from the furniture", so enraptured was he by his idealised world of the forms.

Moore also confuses a complex thing (colour) for a simple thing (yellow). Goodness is in fact a **COMPLEX** idea, like **COLOUR** because it includes within it a whole class of principles we might describe as good (like colour includes, red, yellow, green, blue).

Moore has confused a general category (colour, goodness) for a specific quality of that category (yellowness, generosity).

UTILITARIAN NATURALISM

Utilitarians are normative **NATURALISTS** because they argue that goodness is an observable feature of the natural world - part of our **A POSTERIORI** experience of pleasure and pain. So to work out what is good, we need to project into the future and balance the likely pain and pleasure of our choice. That which maximises happiness and minimises pain is good, and actions that do the opposite are bad.

Utilitarians quite openly commit the **NATURALISTIC FALLACY** (which they argue isn't a fallacy at all) arguing that it is obviously good to pursue happiness because that as a matter of fact is the goal that all humans are pursuing. They give a **TELEOLOGICAL** justification for goodness, just as **NATURAL LAW** theorists such as **AQUINAS** follow Aristotle in linking goodness to **HUMAN FLOURISHING**.

The philosopher **JOHN SEARLE** gives us another naturalist way out of the supposed fallacy. If I promise to pay you £500 then I am doing two things - I am agreeing to play the promising game which involves **OBLIGATION** to pay your money back, and I am accepting that part of the rules of the game, fixed by society, in that I can only break this promise if a large, overriding reason appears for doing so (for example, the money is stolen from me and I am bankrupt, so can't pay it back).

So the making of a promise is a **FACT** but because of the logical feature of promising - that I agree to it creates obligations for me - this allows us to move from a descriptive **IS** statement (Brian owes me £5) to a value **OUGHT** statement "you ought to keep your promise".

AYER's EMOTIVISM ("Expressivism")

A.J. Ayer (1910-1989) formed part of a school of linguistic philosophy called **LOGICAL POSITIVISM** which had at its heart the **VERIFICATION PRINCIPLE**. Truth claims had to be verified true or false by sense-experience. His theory is a theory of **NON-COGNITIVISM** as he argues moral statements add no facts – just opinions which cannot be established true or false empirically. So moral truth cannot be **KNOWN** as objective fact.

> *"The fundamental ethical concepts are unanalysable inasmuch as there is no criterion by which to judge the validity of the judgements. They are mere pseudo-concepts. The presence of an ethical symbol adds nothing to its factual content. Thus if I say to someone 'You acted wrongly in stealing the money,' I am not stating anything more than if I had simply stated 'you stole the money'".* Language, Truth and Logic (1971)

This approach to moral language was a development of **HUME's FORK** - an argument about language developed by David Hume. Hume argued that statements about the real world were of two sorts - they were either analytic or synthetic: either **LOGICAL TRUTHS** or **STATEMENTS OF FACT**.

An analytic statement is true by definition (2 + 2 = 4), a synthetic statement true by experience. So "all bachelors are unmarried" is true by definition, whereas "John is a bachelor" is true by experience (John might be married so that would make the statement **EMPIRICALLY** false). As moral statements are neither analytic (they'd have nothing useful to say about the **REAL** world if they were) or synthetic (not **VERIFIABLE**) they are logically and empirically meaningless.

Ayer put the same point another way.

"The presence of an ethical symbol in a proposition adds nothing to its factual content". (1971:142).

Ayer believed that problems arose when the **NATURALISTS,** such as the **UTILITARIANS** claimed an empirical basis for goodness in the balance of pleasure over pain. What happens when one person's pleasure is another person's pain? Consider that someone steals your wallet. To you, stealing is wrong because it causes you pain. To the thief, stealing is good, because it gives her money to buy food, and she's starving. Stealing appears to be **BOTH** right and wrong at the same time.

This contradictory result indicates there can be no **FACT** of morality – just an **OPINION**.

"It is not self-contradictory to say some pleasant things are not good, or that some bad things are desired". (1971:139)

Ayer means by this that if I say "you were wrong to steal" there is no additional **FACT** introduced by the word "wrong" - only an **EXPRESSION** of a feeling of disapproval. Note he argues the word **GOOD** is not describing a feeling but, in is own words "**EVINCING**" a feeling - like letting out a squeal if you hit your thumb, **"OUCH"**!.

"Stealing money is wrong expresses no proposition which can be either true or false. It's as if I had written "stealing money!!!" where the exclamation marks show a special sort of moral disapproval". A.J. Ayer

EVALUATION OF AYER

Ayer's view seems to be a radical **SUBJECTIVISM** suggesting morality is just "up to me". It seems to strengthen the case for **RELATIVISM** that makes moral debate impossible and disagreements insoluble, even though this is not a theory of **NORMS** but of **MEANING**.

Ayer's view is based on a **FALLACY**. Ludwig Wittgenstein demonstrated that language is part of a game we play with shared rules. **MORAL** language is neither analytic nor synthetic but rather, **PRESCRIPTIVE** as Hare suggests (below). Ayer has committed a fallacy like saying "the world is either square or flat". It's neither.

According to Alasdair MacIntyre in After Virtue, emotivism obliterates the distinction between manipulative and non-manipulative behaviour. There is no longer such an idea as a **VALID REASON**. Moral discourse is simply about manipulating you to adopt my point of view.

ABSOLUTISM and RELATIVISM

Both these are ambiguous ideas. Relativism has three meanings: **PARTICULAR** to culture, **CONSEQUENTIALIST** and **SUBJECTIVE** (up to me).

Absolutism has three meanings which are the opposite: **UNIVERSAL** (applies everywhere and for all time), **NON-CONSEQUENTIALIST** and **OBJECTIVE**.

Theories may not be consistently absolute in all three meanings as the table overleaf demonstrates.

MORAL PROGRESS

Theory	Universal	Non-consequential ist	Objective
Utilitarianism	YES, it claims we all experience pleasure and pain	NO, as goodness is always relative to maximising happiness	YES, as pleasure and happiness are measurable otherwise they couldn't be maximised
Situation Ethics	YES, as we can all understand and live by agape love	NO, as we maximise the value of love	YES, as there is a measurable test for ethical goodness
Kantian Ethics	YES, as we can all universalise a priori	YES, as categorical absolute rules are created	YES, as the Moral Law exists as an objective truth
Natural Law	YES, as we all share one rational human nature	NO, as secondary precepts are applications of reason and never absolute	YES, the world and human nature is set up in certain way - and operates by objective laws

We may therefore conclude that only **KANTIAN** ethics is absolute in all three possible meanings. The other theories have an **ABSOLUTE** element - they have a non-negotiable principle at their heart. That's why Joseph Fletcher calls his theory ~ **PRINCIPLED RELATIVISM** (the absolute principle is **AGAPE**) made relative always to consequences - the second meaning of relativism given earlier.

Is **EMOTIVISM** a form of **RELATIVISM?** It is a meta-ethical theory, not a normative one, and so in one sense the question is a **CATEGORY MISTAKE** as the term can only be applied to the derivation of norms. However, in stressing the absence of **MORAL FACTS** and arguing that moral statements are neither analytic nor synthetic, and therefore meaningless in empirical terms, emotivism does appear to reinforce **SUBJECTIVISM** (our first meaning of relativism).

C.L. STEVENSON's EMOTIVISM (Interest Theory)

Stevenson argued that three criteria must be fulfilled when we use the word "good":

1. We must be able to agree that the action is good.

2. The action must have a **MAGNETISM** - we must want to do it, and feel an **INTEREST** in its being done.

3. The action cannot be verified empirically by appeal to facts.

So moral language has an **EMOTIVE** meaning and a **PERSUASIVE** meaning – we are encouraging others to share our attitude. This is why we bother to **ARGUE** about ethics, whereas on questions of taste we "agree to differ".

> *"Good has an emotive meaning...when a person morally approves of something, he experiences a rich feeling of security when it prospers and is indignant or shocked when it doesn't".*
> *CL Stevenson.*

R.M.HARE's PRESCRIPTIVISM

R.M. Hare (1919-2002) argued that moral judgements have an **EMOTIVE** and a **PRESCRIPTIVE** meaning. This implicitly disagrees with the view of **HUME** and **AYER** who argue that meaningful statements are either analytic (true by definition) or synthetic (true by experience.)

Prescriptions are forms of **IMPERATIVE**: "you oughtn't steal" is equivalent to saying "**DON'T STEAL!**".

Hare agrees that you cannot derive a **PRESCRIPTION** such as "run!" from a description "there's a bull over there!" as there is a **SUBJECTIVE** element (I may choose to walk calmly or stand and wave my red rag). I am free to judge, hence the title of his book **FREEDOM** and **REASON**.

Hare follows **KANT** (even though Hare is a preference utilitarian) in arguing that **REASONABLENESS** lies in the **UNIVERSALISABILITY** of moral statements. Anyone who uses terms like "right" and "ought" are **LOGICALLY COMMITTED** to the idea that any action in relevantly similar circumstances is also wrong (see Kant's first formula of the **CATEGORICAL IMPERATIVE**).

So if Nazis say "Jews must be killed" , they must also judge that if, say it turns out that they are of Jewish origin, then they too must be killed. Only a **FANATIC** would say this.

Hare argues for the importance of **MORAL PRINCIPLES** rather than **RULES**. It is like learning to drive a car:

"The good driver is one whose actions are so exactly governed by principles which have become a habit with him, that he normally does not have to think what to do. But all road

conditions are various, and therefore it is unwise to let all one's
driving become a matter of habit". Language of Morals, page 63

EVALUATION OF PRESCRIPTIVISM

Hare is still denying there are **OBJECTIVE** moral truths. We are free to choose our own principles and determine our actions according to our desires and preferences – there is no objective right and wrong independent of our choosing, but then having chosen, we must be able to universalise it. As a **NON-NATURALIST** he avoids reference to any final **TELOS** such as human flourishing.

Philippa **FOOT** criticised Hare in her lecture in 1958 ("Moral Beliefs") for allowing terribly immoral acts (and people) to be called "moral" simply because they are **CONSISTENT**. We cannot avoid approving the statement "If I was a murderer, I would want to be dead too if I support the death penalty". Prescriptivism cannot help justifying **FANATICISM**.

In his later book **MORAL THINKING** Hare brings together **PRESCRIPTIVISM** and his version of **PREFERENCE UTILITARIANISM**. To prescribe a moral action is to universalise that action – in universalising

"I must take into account all the ideals and preferences held by all those who will be affected and I cannot give any weight to my own ideals. The ultimate effect of this application of universalisability is that a moral judgement must ultimately be based on the maximum possible satisfaction of the preferences of all those affected by it".

Hare's pupil **PETER SINGER** builds on this idea to give prescriptivism an

OBJECTIVE basis in his own version of preference utilitarianism. We are asked to universalise from a neutral, universal viewpoint.

So in the end prescriptivism escapes the charge of being another form of radical **SUBJECTIVISM**.

THE LEGACY OF DAVID HUME

David Hume argued that morality was a matter of acting on desires and feelings. Moral reasoning really reduces to the question "what do I want?" – it remains radically **SUBJECTIVE**. If Hume is right, there is no answer to the question "why should I be moral?" or "why should I be benevolent?". If I don't want to be moral, that seems to be the end of the argument.

J.L. MACKIE (Inventing Right and Wrong,1977) argues that the common view of moral language implies that there are some objective moral facts in the universe. But this view is a **MISTAKE**. There are no moral facts. We can only base our moral judgements on **FEELINGS** and **DESIRES**.

The **INTUITIONISTS** (G.E. Moore, H.A. Prichard, W.D. Ross) are arguing that there are **MORAL FACTS** but that we can only know them **NON-NATURALLY** as internal intuitions. This seems to be an attempt to have our cake and eat it.

R.M. HARE does have an answer to the question "why should I be moral?" At least in his later book **MORAL THINKING**, Hare argues that people are more likely to be happy if they follow universal **PRESCRIPTIVISM** and reason from a viewpoint that takes into account the interests and preferences of all people affected by my decision.

However, this is an appeal to **SELF-INTEREST** – Hare is still an **SUBJECTIVIST**.

NATURAL LAW suggests a **NATURALIST** reason for being moral : we are moral to achieve personal and social **FLOURISHING**. If we can share the insights of psychology and philosophy we can come to a shared (if still **RELATIVISTIC**, cultural) view of what will build the excellent life. Naturalism has undergone a resurgence in the twentieth century, led by Geoffrey **WARNOCK** (1971, The Object of Morality) and Alasdair **MACINTYRE** (1981, After Virtue).

More recent, subtler, attempts to escape **SUBJECTIVISM** are to be found in John **RAWLS'** A Theory of Justice, which asks us to assume the role of an avatar in a space ship, imagining we are in an **ORIGINAL POSITION** heading to a new world where we don't know our gender, intelligence, race, or circumstances. What rules would we formulate for this world? Rawls, like Hare, brings **KANT** back into the forefront of meta-ethical debate.

KEY CONFUSIONS

1. "Utilitarianism is a meta-ethical theory". No, utilitarianism is a **NORMATIVE** theory that is built upon the meta-ethical view that the foundation of morals is **NATURALISTIC** - out there to be observed in the world **A POSTERIORI** (by experience of pleasure and pain). Meta-ethics has nothing to say about exactly how **NORMS** (values of goodness) are derived.

2. "Normative ethics is more useful than meta-ethics". This old exam question has a central ambiguity - more useful for what and to whom? If you're facing a **MORAL DILEMMA**, meta-ethics has no

use at all because it doesn't produce a structure of thought for deciding what to do.

3. "Meta-ethics is boring". This is because it is sometimes badly taught. Actually the structure of morality that builds from meta-ethical **FOUNDATIONS** to **NORMATIVE THEORY** to **PRACTICAL CONCLUSION** is a fascinating one, and we need to think long and hard about how we are to solve moral problems - both **GLOBAL** (war, famine, injustice, poverty, exploitation) and **PERSONAL** (euthanasia, sexual ethics) even though the specification is biased (as in western thought generally) towards the personal.

FUTURE QUESTIONS

1. "The meaning of the word 'good' is the defining question in the study of ethics". Discuss

2. Critically consider whether ethical terms such as good, bad, right and wrong have an objective factual basis that makes them true or false.

3. "Ethical statements are merely an expression of an emotion". Discuss

4. Evaluate the view that ethical statements are meaningless.

5. "People know what's right or wrong by a common sense intuition". Discuss

6. Critically contrast the views of intuitionists and emotivists on the origin and meaning of ethical statements.

KEY QUOTES - META-ETHICS:

1. *"That which is meant by "good" is the only simple object of thought which is peculiar to ethics". G.E. Moore*

2. *"As this ought expresses some new relation it is necessary that it should be observed and explained and at the same time that a reason be given". David Hume*

3. *"The use of "That is bad!" implies an appeal to an objective and impersonal standard in a way in which "I disapprove of this; do so as well!" does not. If emotivism is true, moral language is seriously misleading". Alasdair MacIntyre*

4. *"Good serves only as an emotive sign expressing our attitude to something, and perhaps evoking similar attitudes in other persons". A.J. Ayer*

5. *"To ask whether I ought to do A in these circumstances is to ask whether or not I will that doing A in these circumstances should become a universal law". R.M. Hare*

6. *"We have an idea of good ends that morality serves. Even if we are deontologists, we still think that there is a point to morality, to do with better outcomes – truth-telling generally produces better outcomes than lying. These ends can be put into non-moral language in terms of happiness, flourishing, welfare, or equality". Louis Pojman*

Suggested Reading

Moore, G.E. (1903) Principia Ethica, Chapter II (see peped.org/meta-ethics/extract)

Ayer, A.J. (1936) Language, Truth and Logic, London: Victor Gollancz, Chapter 6 (see peped.org/meta-ethics/extract)

Mackie, J.L. (1977) Ethics: Inventing Right and Wrong, London: Penguin Books, Part 1.3

Conscience

ISSUES

There are four major issues in a study of conscience.

- What is the **ORIGIN** of conscience: does it come from God, our upbringing or from reason?

- Does our conscience and sense of right and wrong emerge in childhood as a result of parental praise and blame? Is guilt a product of certain complexes, such as Freud's **OEDIPUS COMPLEX?**

- What is conscience, how does it **WORK**: is it a **MENTAL PROCESS** or part of our **REASON**, or a **FEELING**, or a **VOICE** in our heads (the voice of God?)?

- Can we go against our conscience and choose to reject it, in other words, is conscience **FALLIBLE** and so likely to make mistakes, or is it inerrant (incapable of error)? What is the relationship between conscience and human **WILL**?

SPECIFICATION

Requires us to consider **FREUD**'s Psychological approach and **AQUINAS'** Theological Approach, to compare and critically evaluate these two theories. We are at liberty to contrast them with Eric **FROMM**,

BUTLER or **NEWMAN** or anyone else - the syllabus is open-ended about additional material. We do, however, need to compare and contrast them with philosophers/authors of a different persuasion - so these are included in this guide. Students need to decide which is most relevant to their own approach of critical analysis and evaluation of Aquinas and Freud.

THE PSYCHOLOGY OF CONSCIENCE – SIGMUND FREUD

BACKGROUND

ENLIGHTENMENT – believed in reason and measurement but also hypothesis tested **A POSTERIORI.** Freud shared this belief that science could probe the deepest unconscious recesses of the human mind and so contribute to the advancement of human welfare.

- **COPERNICUS** taught us that humans were not the centre of the universe.

- **DARWIN** taught us that humans were just another species of animal.

- **FREUD** taught us that humans were not rational actors, but rather are driven by unconscious, primitive, instinctual desires.

KEY TERMS

CATEGORICAL IMPERATIVE unconditional demands of the superego whose violation produces guilt

CONSCIENCE The part of human consciousness that guides moral decisions and equivalent to the superego

EGO The part of the human mind that forms our idea of self and presents a coherent image to the outside world. The ego longs for a moral guide.

ID The part of the human mind which processes passions and emotions. It is non-moral and is often in conflict with ego and superego.

SUPEREGO The part of the human mind which regulates behaviour, formed in childhood by relationships with authority figures (father and mother) and by praise and blame.

REPRESSION The suppression of our real emotions because they do not conform to ego-identity or are categorized as shameful by the superego.

EROS The creative life-force which is also the mischief-maker as it encourages the ego to take risks and cross boundaries.

THANATOS The death-instinct in conflict with eros, which appears in destructive patterns of behaviour (self-harm, aggression, and even suicide).

UNCONSCIOUS That part of the iceberg of the human mind which lies unseen but nonetheless influences and even controls behaviour.

LIBIDO The sexual instinct which forms part of eros and is often repressed or overly controlled by the superego.

NEUROSIS Mental illness which results from a failure to create a coherent and harmonious ego. Examples might be hysteria, obsessive-compulsive disorders (e.g. washing rituals) and phobias (e.g. fear of spiders).

GUILT Feelings of shame arising from the authority of the superego and the conflict with the id. Guilt can be suppressed and form part of the unconscious.

BACKGROUND

Sigmund Freud (1856-1939) is the **FATHER OF PSYCHOANALYSIS** through his theories of how the conscious and unconscious mind develop and interact. He believed in the **ENLIGHTENMENT** assumption that science could understand all aspects of human behaviour by observing **A POSTERIORI** how patients respond to **PSYCHOANALYSIS** and by positing **THEORIES** (such as **EGO, ID** and **SUPEREGO**) which provide a **STRUCTURE** of thinking.

CONSCIENCE for Freud was a product of experiences in childhood which result in the creation of a **SUPEREGO** – an internal guide which seeks to calm our fears, order our world and resolve conflicts between **EGO** and **ID**. The conscience (superego) is the representative of the voice of our parents who in early childhood produced feelings of pleasure (approval/being loved) and pain (shame/punishment). Various attachments either dissolve (the **OEDIPUS COMPLEX**) or strengthen (gender identification with mother or father), and failure to reconcile a feeling of inner conflict or suppressed desire can lead to depression and **NEUROSIS**.

The structure of Freud's thinking is given on the opposite page, and his theory is sometimes referred to as a **STRUCTURAL THEORY** of the human mind and consciousness. He explains behaviour in terms of the **UNCONSCIOUS** and the sublimation of desire (for example in ideas of God as **FATHER**), or the repression of desire (such as the **LIBIDO** or sexual desire).

STRUCTURE OF THOUGHT

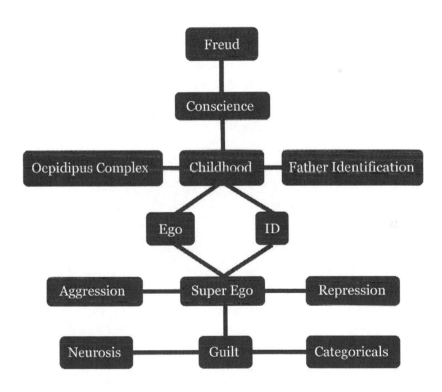

EGO

The child develops a sense of **SELF** in relation to the external world. The **EGO** experiences feelings of pleasure and pain and also conscious and unconscious **DESIRES**. The pain of experience propels us towards change but can arise out of **REPRESSION** of urges which become unconscious.

The sense of self begins in childhood with an **IDENTIFICATION** with either **FATHER** or **MOTHER**. The origins of the relationship with the **MOTHER** are explained by the **OEDIPUS COMPLEX** and with the **FATHER** by a process by which the father (**AUTHORITY FIGURE**) becomes part of the infantile stage of the **SUPEREGO**.

CARL JUNG also proposed an **ELECTRA COMPLEX** in 1913 to explain a girl's psychosexual competition with her mother for possession of her father.

The **EGO** thus assumes a regulatory role - it excludes feelings and memories which don't fit our idea of self. For example, this repression resurfaces in **DREAMS** and also **PHOBIAS** – a fear of spiders, for example, which reflect unconscious sources of anxiety. Freud believed the **EGO** was striving to be moral.

The role of **PSYCHOANALYSIS** is to seek to integrate the "coherent ego and the repressed self which is split off from it" (Freud).

Our behaviour (**ACTION**) is a product of both conscious choices and **UNCONSCIOUS** forces 'which exert a driving force without the **EGO** noticing the compulsion" (Freud). These forces result in behaviour which are driven by a complex **PSYCHIC ENERGY** which can leave the human being baffled and confused by their own behaviour – resulting in a feeling of **ANXIETY** or **GUILT**, and **DEPRESSION** (which Freud called 'melancholia').

ID

The **ID** is the seat of feelings, and passions. It is totally non-moral. The origin of the **ID** lies in our **EVOLUTIONARY** background but also in society itself which has conditioned us over generations.

The **ID** develops two broad categories of desire, according to Freud. **EROS** is the life-instinct, which gives us the desires for food, self-preservation, and sex. **THANATOS** is the death-instinct, which drives desires for domination, aggression, violence and self-destruction. These two instincts are at war within the id, and need to be tempered by ego constraints and by **CONSCIENCE**.

Children learn that authorities in the world restrict the extent to which these desires are satisfied. Consequently, humans create the **EGO** which takes account of the realities of the world and society. The ego Freud referred to as the **REALITY PRINCIPLE**, because our awareness of self and of others is crucial to our interaction with the world around us, and is formed at the age of 3 to 5 years.

Within the **ID** there is a battle going on between **EROS** – the life instinct – and **THANATOS** – the death instinct. **EROS** is the 'mischief-maker' (Freud) – the source of uncontrolled passion and also creativity. It is dominated by the **PLEASURE PRINCIPLE**, and yet not all pleasures are felt as acceptable or 'good'. Hence the irrational guilt that can occur over, for example, masturbation and its presence as a **TABOO** in Christianity. Indeed, **EROS** is often at odds with the demands and **CATEGORICAL IMPERATIVES** (Freud's phrase echoing Kant) of the **SUPEREGO**.

The death-instinct (**THANATOS**) is experienced in the desire to kill the **FATHER** and replace him in the mother's affections in the **OEDIPUS COMPLEX**, but is also present in the destructive desires of the **DEPRESSIVE** or self-harming **NEUROTIC**. The death instinct also emerges in **AGGRESSION**, violence and war. In the individual it can have its final expression in **SUICIDE**. But is the positing of a sexual complex just pseudo-science?

SUPEREGO

The **SUPEREGO** represents the **INTERNAL** world of **CONSCIENCE**. "The superego represents the relationship to our parents" (Freud) and particularly our **FATHER** as authority figure and source of rules and punishments.

To Freud there is a conflict within the human psyche between **EGO** and **ID** and **EROS** and **THANATOS**. A sense of dread emerges in childhood from a fear of castration, a fear of death and a fear of **SEPARATION** from our parents, particularly a fear of loss of the mother's love. The superego can have a destructive power: causing the **EGO** to feel deserted and unloved, abandoned to an anxious and uncertain world and 'fuelling the death-instinct by making the Ego feel abandoned'. This sense of abandonment and powerlessness resurfaces in **DREAMS** (often of failure or of loss of control).

So the **SUPEREGO** can have both a **POSITIVE** and a **NEGATIVE** role – positive in controlling unbridled and anti-social desires and passions, but also **NEGATIVE** in forming an extreme critical voice "brutally chastising and punishing" with guilt, or shame and ultimately a sense of **SELF-HATRED** which cause self-harm and depression.

We can also experience the **SUPEREGO** as **SAVIOUR** and project our guilt and shame onto a sense of **SIN** and a **FATHER-FIGURE** – whom we call **GOD**, who replaces lost love and provides a **SUBLIMATION** of our sexual desires. Christianity teaches that we deserve death, but that our place is taken by a substitute, Jesus Christ, who removes the **GUILT** and takes on himself the **PUNISHMENT.** (Isaiah 53 "the punishment that makes us whole is upon him").

The **SUPEREGO** in this way grows into a life and power of its own irrespective of the rational thought and reflection of the individual: it is programmed into us by the reactions of other people.

This 'superego', conscience, restricts humans' aggressive powerful desires **(THANATOS** within the id) which would otherwise **DESTROY** us. So guilt "expresses itself in the need for punishment" (Civilisation and its Discontents 1930:315-6). **ERIC FROMM**, quoting Nietzsche, agrees with Freud's analysis of the destructive nature of the **AUTHORITARIAN** conscience.

"Freud has convincingly demonstrated the correctness of Nietzsche's thesis that the blockage of freedom turns man's instincts 'backward against man himself'. Enmity, cruelty, the delight in persecution...- the turning of all these instincts against their own possessors: this is the origin of the bad conscience".
Eric Fromm, Man For Himself, 1947:113

Our superego can lead us to **INTERNALISE** shame, and to experience conflicts between the id desires and the shame emanating from the superego responses. The more we suppress our true feelings, the more that which drives us comes from what Freud described as the **SUBCONSCIOUS**, which like an iceberg lies hidden in the recesses of our minds.

GUILT

Freud believed that the more rapidly the **OEDIPUS COMPLEX** succumbed to **REPRESSION** of our desire for our mother, the stronger will be the domination of the **SUPEREGO** over the **EGO** in the form of a severe and dictatorial **CONSCIENCE**.

So "the tension between the demands of conscience and the actual performances of the ego is experienced in a sense of guilt" (Freud). But guilt can itself be **REPRESSED** and so **UNCONSCIOUS**. Unconscious guilt expresses itself in **NEUROSIS** and other forms of **MENTAL ILLNESS**.

SYNOPTIC POINT Freud sees the structure of our Psyche much as Plato describes it in the analogy of the Charioteer (reason) who seeks to harmonise the twin horses of virtue and passion. A man on horseback (the **EGO**) tries to hold in check the superior strength of the horse (**ID**). But unlike the horseman, the **EGO** uses forces borrowed from the **SUPEREGO** – such as shame and guilt. But a result of this is that **EGO**-identity increasingly fails to represent **ID**-desire. The unfulfilled **ID** resurfaces in sick behaviour or **UNCONSCIOUS** forces (**COMPULSIONS**).

OEDIPUS COMPLEX

Oedipus so loved his mother that he killed his father and assumed his father's role. Infants start with **MOTHER-ATTACHMENT** which is reinforced by the **PLEASURE PRNCIPLE** as the mother satisfies the infants need for sustenance, love and erotic feeling. The hostility to the **FATHER** gradually subsides in healthy children who become more fully identified with the **MOTHER** (girls) or the **FATHER** (boys) as puberty approaches.

However, a failure to identify successfully with one or other parent can lead to transfer of love (Freud saw this as the origin of **HOMOSEXUAL LOVE**). The **EGO** deepens its relationship with the **ID** in rituals which may be associated with shame, such as masturbation, and fantasies that produce guilt. So the **LIBIDO** can be redirected or even suppressed altogether in a sublimation which we call **RELIGION**.

Ultimately, to Freud, Religion is an infantile projection of our desires and longings onto an image which is an **ILLUSION**. In the Christian Thought paper we study more of this theory in Freud's work, The Future of an Illusion.

EVALUATING FREUD

Weaknesses

REDUCTIONIST George Klein (1973) argues Freud reduces the human mind to an object of enquiry by positing unprovable theories of how conscious and unconscious processes interact. In so doing he reduces human behaviour to a dualism of 'appropriate' and 'inappropriate' behaviour. Like the criticism levelled at geneticist **RICHARD DAWKINS**

we can see this as a form of scientific reductionism.

OVERSEXUALISED Freud argues that the relationship of child and parent has sexual desire through the development of the **OEDIPUS COMPEX** as a key factor. The success or failure of a child's sexual feelings for one or other parent as key to child development is highly contentious. For example, a boy's father is his mother's lover, but he's also the disciplinarian. So, assuming boys do harbour feelings of fear toward their fathers, is this because they fear castration by a romantic rival or because they're afraid of ordinary punishment?

SAMPLING Freud's sample is primarily Austrian upper-class woman, who manifested hysteria. The sample is too small and gender-biased to be truly scientific and the emphasis on sex reveals the cultural repression of that age. Scholars argue Freud fabricates the claim that "almost all of my women patients told me that they had been seduced by their father". John Kihlstrom comments: "While Freud had an enormous impact on 20th century culture, he has been a dead weight on 20th century psychology. The broad themes that Westen writes about were present in psychology before Freud, or arose more recently, independent of his influence. At best, Freud is a figure of only historical interest for psychologists".

Strengths

REVOLUTIONARY Freud was the first person to analyse and theorise about the human unconscious. His argument that dreams are a key to unlocking the secrets of the subconscious mind, his belief that hypnotherapy could change behaviour and his invention of **TALKING THERAPIES** have fundamentally changed our treatment of mental illness.

SECULAR Freud believed religion was a neurosis based on delusions and projections – for example God is a father-substitute onto whom we project our desire for an authority figure, our fear of death and our sense of abandonment. This to Freud was infantile. Westen (1998:35) argues "the notion of unconscious processes is not psychoanalytic voodoo, and it is not the fantasy of muddle-headed clinicians. It is not only clinically indispensable, but it is good science".

HUMANE Freud treated the whole human personality rather than condemning aspects of it as shameful, evil or unacceptable. He thereby challenged the old religious **DUALISMS** of good versus evil, monster versus hero, to give a humane alternative and offering hope of cure and transformation to those whose lives were blighted by mental health problems.

KEY QUOTES - FREUD

1. *"In the Ego and the Id Freud abandons the simple dichotomy between instinct and consciousness and recognizes the unconscious elements of the ego and superego, the importance of nonsexual impulses (aggression or the 'death instinct'), and the alliance between superego and id, superego and aggression". Christopher Lasch The Culture of Narcissism page 32*

2. *"While Freud had an enormous impact on 20th century culture, he has been a dead weight on 20th century psychology. The broad themes were present in psychology before Freud, or arose in more recently independent of his influence. At best, Freud is a figure of only historical interest for psychologists." John Kihlstrom*

3. *"When we were little children we knew these higher natures of our parents, and later we took them into ourselves"*. Freud

3. *"All that is repressed is unconscious, but not all that is unconscious is repressed"*. Freud

4. *"To the ego, living means the same as being loved"*. Freud

5. *"By setting up the superego, the ego has mastered the Oedipus Complex and placed itself in subjection to the Id"*. Freud

6. *"The tension between the demands of conscience and the performance of the ego is experienced as guilt"*. Freud

7. *"As the child was once under the domination of its parents, so the ego submits to the Categorical Imperative of the superego"*. Freud

8. *"Human megalomania will have suffered its third and most wounding blow from the psychological research of the present time which seeks to prove to the ego that it is not even master in its own house"*. Freud

PIAGET AND CHILD DEVELOPMENT

Later psychologists modified Freud's theory. They argued that conscience has a mature and immature dimension.

MATURE conscience is healthy and is identified with the ego's search for integrity. It is concerned with right and wrong, and acts dynamically and responsively on things of value.

The mature conscience looks **OUTWARDS** to the world and the future, developing new insights into situations.

The **IMMATURE** conscience comprises the mass of guilty feelings acquired from parental and school discipline. These feelings have little to do with the rational importance of the action. The immature conscience acts out a desire to seek **APPROVAL** from others instead of the principles and beliefs of the person.

Piaget experimented to try to discover how conscience develops. He found that up to the age of ten, children judge rightness or wrongness according to the **CONSEQUENCES** of an action (eg I pile baked bean tins behind a door, as they crash down they make a terrible noise. The younger child feels guilty). Older children begin to link rightness and wrongness with **MOTIVE** and intention. In the above example, the child did not want or intend to scatter the baked bean cans, so the older child reasons "I'm not guilty!"

EVALUATION

These psychological accounts of conscience undermine **AQUINAS'** religious theory of conscience (see below) because conscience is **ENVIRONMENTALLY INDUCED** by upbringing, not innate.

Freud's theory is highly **DETERMINISTIC**, because humans are driven, according to Freud, by forces operating out of our subconscious minds.

PSYCHOLOGY doesn't rule out the possibility that God has some involvement with conscience (in originating a moral faculty, for example), but if environment operates so strongly on conscience the religious theories need reworking.

A THEOLOGY OF CONSCIENCE - AQUINAS

KEY TERMS

CONSCIENTIA Aquinas' definition of conscience as 'reason mag right decisions".

SYNDERESIS Aquinas' definition of conscience as our innate ability and desire to orientate ourselves towards good ends (**PRIMARY PRECEPTS**).

PHRONESIS Practical wisdom or right judgement.

VINCIBLE IGNORANCE Blameworthy ignorance of something which we should in principle know about eg a 30 mph zone.

INVINCIBLE IGNORANCE Ignorance which we can't be blamed for - eg a Borneo tribesman's ignorance of Jesus Christ.

St Paul argued that all human beings, Jew and Gentile (non-Jew), possessed an **INNATE** knowledge of God's law, (we're born with it) written on our hearts. "I do not do the thing I want, the very thing I hate is what I do" he wrote in **ROMANS 7** and Gentiles have God's law "engraved on their hearts", (Romans 2:15).

John Henry **NEWMAN** (1801-1890) was an Anglican priest who converted to Rome. How could a good Catholic accept papal **INFALLIBILITY** and still follow his conscience? Newman describes conscience as the innate **VOICE OF GOD** and **ABORIGINAL** (= original or native) **VICAR OF CHRIST**.

"It is a principle planted in us before we have had any training" argued Newman. *Newman quoted the fourth Lateran Council when he said "he who acts against conscience loses his soul".*
John Henry Newman

Aquinas (1224-1274) agrees with St Paul and with Newman, as he distinguished between an innate source of good and evil, **SYNDERESIS** (literally, one who watches over us) and a judgement derived from our reason, **CONSCIENTIA**. This second idea is, however, closer to **JOSEPH BUTLER**.

STRUCTURE OF THOUGHT

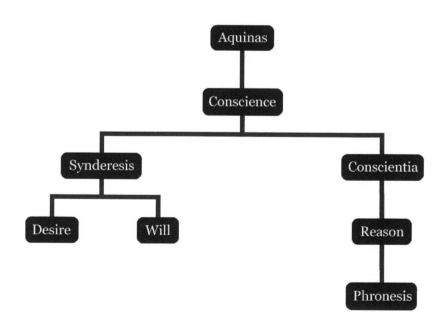

SYNDERESIS and CONSCIENTIA

Thomas Aquinas saw **SYNDERESIS** (first of two words for conscience) as an innate instinct for distinguishing right from wrong that orientates **DESIRE** and forms the **WILL**. Synderesis can be defined as:

"A natural disposition of the human mind by which we instinctively understand the first principles of morality". Aquinas

Aquinas (optimistically) thought people tended towards goodness and away from evil (the **SYNDERESIS** principle). This principle is the starting point or **FIRST PRINCIPLE** of Aquinas' **NATURAL LAW** system of ethics. So these 'first principles' are the **PRIMARY PRECEPTS** which we observe rational human beings pursue as goals. These include preservation of life, ordered society, worship of God, education and reproduction (acronym **POWER**).

CONSCIENTIA is the power of reason for working out what is good and what is evil, the "application of knowledge to activity" (Aquinas). This is something closer to moral judgement rather than instinct, close to Aristotle's **PHRONESIS** or practical wisdom or **BUTLER**'s determining processs for distinguishing between **SELF-INTEREST** and **BENEVOLENCE**. We cannot flourish without it. In practical situations we have to make choices and to weigh alternatives, and we do so by using our conscience. One way we do this is by looking at consequences and applying the **PRINCIPLE OF DOUBLE EFFECT** (when we have to kill a foetus to save a mother's life we have a good intention but a double effect of one good and one evil consequence).

Conscience can make mistakes and needs to be trained in wisdom. At times people do bad things because they make a mistake in discriminating good from evil. Aquinas believed that if the conscience has made a **FACTUAL** mistake, for example, if I don't realise that my action breaks a particular rule, then my mistaken conscience is not to blame.

But if I am simply **IGNORANT** of the rule (such as not committing adultery), I am to blame. Taking a rather bizarre example, Aquinas argues that if a man sleeps with another man's wife thinking she was his wife, then he is not morally blameworthy because he acted "in good faith"."Conscience is reason making right decisions and not a voice giving us commands". Aquinas

Conscience deliberates between good and bad. Aquinas notes two dimensions of moral decision making, "Man's reasoning is a kind of movement which begins with the understanding of certain things that are naturally known as **IMMUTABLE** principles without investigation. It ends in the intellectual activity by which we make judgements on the basis of those principles". Aquinas

So Synderesis is right **INSTINCT** or habit, the natural tendency humans have to do good and avoid evil. Conscientia is right **REASON**, which distinguishes between right and wrong as we make practical moral decisions. We see how conscientia works itself out in the **PRINCIPLE OF DOUBLE EFFECT,** when we solve a genuine moral dilemma, when two 'good things' conflict and we can't have both.

VINCIBLE and INVINCIBLE IGNORANCE

INVINCIBLE IGNORANCE occurs when people (such as non-Christians or tribes in Borneo) are ignorant of the moral law not because they refuse to believe, but rather because they've not yet had an opportunity to hear and experience it. St. Thomas Aquinas discusses the topic in his Summa Theologica 1-1 Q97. Pope Pius IX used the term in his 1854 document Singulari Quadam .

In his 1963 sermon, "Strength to Love," Martin Luther King wrote, "Nothing in all the world is more dangerous than sincere ignorance and conscientious stupidity." Intentional **VINCIBLE** ignorance is when I deliberately act on ignorance. For example, if I choose to fire my rifle into a forest without first making sure there's no-one in the undergrowth picking blackberries, I am "vincibly" ignorant and morally culpable for my actions.

JOSEPH BUTLER – INNATE CONSCIENCE THAT IS GUIDED BY REASON

Butler (1692-1752), former Bishop of Durham, believed human beings had two natural rational guides to behaviour: enlightened self-interest and conscience. Greeks like **EPICURUS** would have recognised the self-interest of the pursuit of **HAPPINESS**, but not the idea of an **INNATE** (inborn) disposition of conscience.

Butler believed we were naturally moral, and that conscience was the **SUPREME AUTHORITY** in moral actions. Morality was part of our human natures.

Human nature has a **HIERARCHY OF VALUES** with conscience at the top which than adjudicates between the self-love and **BENEVOLENCE** (= doing good to others) which define us as human beings. Conscience helps the selfish human become virtuous and so provides a **BALANCE** between these two tendencies.

Butler doesn't deny we have feelings and passions, but it is conscience which **JUDGES** between them as the "moral approving and disapproving faculty" and we act **PROPORTIONATELY** (appropriately to the situation) according to our conscience.

The guidance is **INTUITIVE**, given by God but still the voice of **REASON**. He is arguing that each human being has direct insight into the **UNIVERSAL** or objective rightness or wrongness of an action.

EVALUATION OF BUTLER

Butler attacked the **EGOISM** of Thomas Hobbes. **BENEVOLENCE** is as much part of our shared human nature as **SELF-LOVE**. Here there are echoes of Richard **DAWKINS'** argument that we all share a biologically evolved "altruistic gene" (altruism = concern for others).

Butler sees an **OBJECTIVE MORAL ORDER** in the world. Fortune and misfortune are not entirely arbitrary – if we choose **VICE** we naturally suffer misfortune. Following the dictates of conscience usually leads to **HAPPINESS**. But in the end it's **GOD** who guarantees the consequences turn out best.

"Although Butler's description of conscience is **UNSURPASSED**, he gives no definition of conscience". D.D.Raphael

> *"Common behaviour all over the world is formed on a supposition of a moral faculty; whether called conscience, moral reason, moral sense, or divine reason; whether considered as a sentiment of understanding, or as a perception of the heart".*
> *Joseph Butler*

JOHN HENRY NEWMAN AND CONSCIENCE

Cardinal John Henry Newman also took an **INTUITIONIST** approach. He wrote that "conscience is a law of the mind ... a messenger of him, who, both in nature and in grace, speaks to us behind a veil, and teaches and rules us by his representatives. Conscience is the aboriginal (ie original or natural) vicar of Christ." (John Henry Cardinal Newman, Letter to the Duke of Norfolk).

Newman believed that following conscience was following **DIVINE LAW**. Conscience is a messenger from God, and it is God speaking to us. Newman was a devout Catholic, but said in a letter 'I toast the Pope, but I toast conscience first'.

Catholics are obliged to do what they **SINCERELY BELIEVE** to be right even if they are mistaken. In a commentary to the Vatican documents, a brilliant young theologian named Joseph Ratzinger (now Pope Benedict) seems to agree.

"Over the Pope as the expression of the binding claim of ecclesiastical authority there still stands one's own conscience, which must be obeyed before all else, if necessary even against the requirement of ecclesiastical authority". Pope Benedict

What happens where individual conscience comes up against **MORAL ABSOLUTES**, such as the absolute condemnation of abortion and contraception. The Church teaches that using artificial contraception is intrinsically wrong because it breaks the **INTRINSIC** link between sex and reproduction. Yet many couples ignore this teaching and maintain the inherent goodness of birth control to limit population growth, or maintain choices over careers.

So the Roman Catholic Church's teaching on conscience reflects both Newman and Aquinas and it holds that conscience is the law that speaks to the heart: 'conscience is a law written by God', (Papal encyclical, Gaudium et Spes).

AUTHORITARIAN CONSCIENCE: ERIC FROMM

Eric Fromm experienced all the evil of Nazism and wrote his books to reflect on how conscience and freedom can be subverted even in the most civilised societies. In order to explain how, for example, Adolf **EICHMANN** can plead at his trial for mass murder in 1961 that he was only "following orders" in applying the final solution, we can invoke Fromm's idea of the authoritarian conscience.

The authoritarian conscience is the **INTERNALISED VOICE** of the external authority, something close to Freud's concept of the superego considered above. It's backed up by fear of punishment, or spurred on by admiration or can even be created because I idolise an authority figure, as Unity **MITFORD** did Adolf Hitler.

As Unity found, this blinds us to the faults of the idolised figure, and causes us to become **SUBJECT** to that person's will, so that "the laws and sanctions of the externalised authority become part of oneself" (1947:108).

So, as with the Nazis, ordinary seemingly civilised human beings do **ATROCIOUS EVIL** because they are subject to a voice which comes essentially from outside them, bypassing their own moral sense. This authoritarian conscience can come from:

PROJECTION onto someone of an image of perfection.

The experience of parental **RULES** or expectations.

An adopted **BELIEF** system, such as a religion, with its own authority structure.

> *"Good conscience is consciousness of pleasing authority, guilty conscience is consciousness of displeasing it".* Eric Fromm *(1947:109)*

The individual's **IDENTITY** and sense of security has become wrapped up in the authority figure, and the voice inside is really someone else's voice. This also means **OBEDIENCE** becomes the cardinal virtue, and as the Nazi Adolf Eichmann pleaded at his trial. **AUTONOMY** and **CREATIVITY** are lost.

> *"Those subject to him are means to his end and, consequently his property, and used by him for his purposes."* Fromm *(1947:112)*

DESTRUCTIVE TENDENCIES emerge, Fromm stresses, where "a person takes on the role of authority by treating himself with the same cruelty and strictness" and "destructive energies are discharged by taking on the role of the authority and dominating oneself as servant". (1947:113)

> *"Paradoxically, authoritarian guilty conscience is a result of feelings of strength, independence, productiveness and pride, while the authoritarian good conscience springs from feelings of obedience, dependence, powerlessness and sinfulness".* Fromm *(1947:112)*

THE HUMANISTIC CONSCIENCE

The **HUMANISTIC** conscience, Fromm suggests is "our own voice, present in every human being, and independent of external sanctions and rewards" (1947:118). Fromm sees this voice as our **TRUE SELVES**, found by listening to ourselves and heeding our deepest needs, desires and goals.

> *"Different from the authoritarian conscience is the "humanistic conscience"; this is the voice present in every human being and independent from external sanctions and rewards. Humanistic conscience is based on the fact that as human beings we have an intuitive knowledge of what is human and inhuman, what is conducive of life and what is destructive of life. This conscience serves our functioning as human beings. It is the voice which calls us back to ourselves, to our humanity".* Eric Fromm

The result of so listening is to release **HUMAN POTENTIAL** and creativity, and to become what we potentially are; "the goal is productiveness, and therefore, happiness" (1947:120). This is something gained over a life of learning, reflection and setting and realising goals for ourselves.

Fromm sees **KAFKA**'s "The Trial" as a parable of how the two consciences in practice live together. A man is arrested, he knows not on what charge or pretext. He seems powerless to prevent a terrible fate - his own death - at the hands of this alien authority. But just before he dies he gains a glimpse of another person (Fromm's more developed **HUMANISTIC CONSCIENCE**) looking at him from an upstairs room.

KEY CONFUSIONS

1. "Conscience is a form of consciousness". No, conscience is only a form of consciousness if it is clearly an exercise of choice and reason, as in Aquinas' **CONSCIENTIA** or Butler's principle of judgement between self-interest and benevolence. But Freud argues **UNCONSCIOUS** forces drive guilt feelings which drive conscience - and these forces may be irrational or **NEUROTIC**.

2. "Without God there can be no human conscience". Only in a certain (narrow) Christian world view that sees even our moral sense corrupted by sin. To Aquinas we all share in **SYNDERESIS** which means conscience is a **UNIVERSAL** phenomenon we possess by virtue of our creation in the **IMAGE OF GOD**. It doesn't matter if we believe in God or not.

3. "Science cannot explain conscience". Richard **DAWKINS** would disagree. The **SELFISH GENE** is actually the **SELF-PRESERVING** gene and evolution has given us a genetic predisposition to **ALTRUISM**. So when the conscience of a distinguished Leeds surgeon caused him to jump into the surf off Cornwall to try to save two teenaged swimmers in distress in 2015, he was showing the **ALTRUISTIC** (help others) gene. He tragically died in this heroic moral action.

FUTURE QUESTIONS

1. Critically evaluate the theories of conscience of Aquinas and Freud.

2. "Conscience is given by God, not formed by childhood experience". Critically evaluate this view with reference to Freud and Aquinas.

3. "Conscience is a product of culture, environment, genetic predisposition and education". Discuss

4. "Conscience is another word for irrational feelings of guilt". Discuss

5. "Freud's theory of conscience has no scientific basis. It is merely hypothesis". Discuss

6. 'Guilt feelings are induced by social relationships as a method of control". Discuss

KEY QUOTES - CONSCIENCE

1. *"Freud has convincingly demonstrated the correctness of Nietzsche's thesis that the blockage of freedom turns man's instincts 'backward against man himself'. Enmity, cruelty, the delight in persecution - the turning of all these instincts against their own possessors: this is the origin of the bad conscience".* *Eric Fromm*

2. *"Conscience does not only offer itself to show us the way we should walk in, but it likewise carries its own authority with it, that it is our natural guide, the guide assigned us by the Author*

of our nature; it therefore belongs to our condition of being, it is our duty to walk in its path". Joseph Butler

3. *"Conscience is reason making right decisions and not a voice giving us commands". Aquinas*

4. *"The Gentiles can demonstrate the effects of the law engraved on their hearts, to which their own conscience bears witness". Rom 2.15*

5. *"Conscience is the built in monitor of moral action or choice values". John Macquarrie*

Suggested Reading

Aquinas Summa Theologica 1-1 Q79 (see peped.org/conscience/extracts)

Freud, S. The Ego and the Id Createspace Independent Publishing Platform (22 Mar. 2010)

Fromm, E. (1947) Man for Himself: An Inquiry into the Psychology of Ethics London: Routledge, IV.2

Internet Encyclopaedia of Philosophy, Sigmund Freud, http://www.iep.utm.edu/freud/ (See peped.org/conscience/extracts)

Kihlstrom, John F. (2015). Personality (Pearson) and The Psychological Unconscious. In L.R. Pervin & O. John (Eds.), Handbook of personality, 2nd ed. (pp. 424-442). New York: Guilford. http://socrates.berkeley.edu/~kihlstrm/PersonalityWeb/Ch8CritiquePsychoanalysis.htm

Macmillan, M.B. (1996).Freud evaluated: The completed arc. Cambridge, Ma.: MIT Press.

Strohm, P. (2011) Conscience: A Very Short Introduction, Oxford University Press, Chapters 1 and 3

Westen, D. (1998). The Scientific Legacy of Sigmund Freud. Psychological Bulletin,124, 333-371

Sexual Ethics

ISSUES SURROUNDING SEXUAL ETHICS

What does it mean to be **HUMAN**? Is there one **UNIVERSAL** shared human nature (as Natural Law suggests)?

Are gender equality and same sex attraction equally ethical issues? Or is it just a matter of the consequences of social policy and individual action, as the Utilitarians suggest?

What values give meaning to sexual relationships (such as fidelity, chastity, commitment – which seem to be changing)? Are the **VIRTUES** of human character a better way of analysing this issue?

How have developments in understanding the biology and **PSYCHOLOGY** of the human person affected sexual ethics?

Sexual ethics thus shares concerns and insights from **PSYCHOLOGY**, **BIOLOGY**, and **SOCIOLOGY**. With the prevalence of pornography, sex trafficking and decline in old models of family life, there can be few more pressing ethical issues facing us. The specification identifies three issues:

- **PRE-MARITAL SEX**

- **EXTRA-MARITAL SEX (ADULTERY)**

- **HOMOSEXUALITY**

STRUCTURE OF THOUGHT

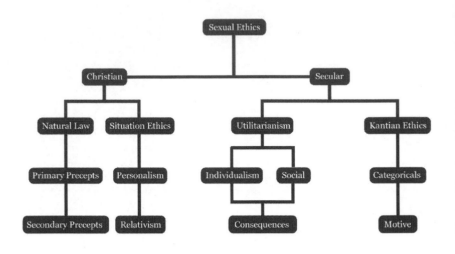

SEX AND EVOLUTION

Homo Sapiens emerged around 150,000 years ago. As social life developed so a primitive **MORALITY** created rules and boundaries around sexual intercourse. Sex changes its function from **REPRODUCTION** to **SOCIAL REGULATION**.

Religions emerge that created **PURITY CODES**. These involved **TABOOS** (the declaration of certain practices as unclean). For example the purity code of the Hebrew Bible, **LEVITICUS**, lays down a code of uncleanness – which included **BLOOD**, **INCEST**, **ADULTERY**, and **SAME SEX RELATIONS**. These are abominations punishable by social exclusion or death.

Such attitudes are reflected in attitudes to **WOMEN**. Women came to be seen as **PROPERTY** of men. Virginity was prized. Up to 1872, married women in Britain had to surrender all property to their husbands; there was no concept of marital rape until 1991 and violence against married women was only outlawed in 1861. In 2011 there were 443 reported incidents of "honour crime" (violence, forced marriage and even murder) in the UK.

A concept of what is **NATURAL** emerged and with it psychological **GUILT** for those who did not conform. It's hard to believe that in 1899 **OSCAR WILDE** was jailed for two years hard labour for a homosexual relationship. **HOMOSEXUAL SEX** was only legalised in 1967. The last people to be executed for sodomy in England were James Pratt (1805–1835) and John Smith (1795–1835), in November 1835.

KINSEY AND THE SEXUAL REVOLUTION

The Kinsey report of 1945 shocked America. Intimate surveys of real people's preferences revealed:

- 10% of men were homosexual for at least three years of their lives. How then could sexual preference be **UNCHANGING**, fixed and uniform?

- 26% of married women had extramarital experiences of different sorts.

- 90% of men masturbated.

- 50% of men had been unfaithful to their wives.

CHRISTIAN VIEW OF SEX

NATURAL LAW

Aquinas taught that there were three rational ends of sex, arising from the **PRIMARY PRECEPT** of reproduction:

- To have children.

- To give **PLEASURE**.

- To bind husband and wife together.

His view – that sex was for pleasure, was widely condemned, Aquinas wrote "the exceeding pleasure experienced in sex does not destroy the balance of nature as long as it is in harmony with reason". Right reason involves a delicate balance of the three purposes of sex – and avoidance of irrational or animal extremes. So the following sexual sins were forbidden:

- **RAPE**

- **CASUAL SEX**

- **ADULTERY**

- **HOMOSEXUAL SEX**

- **MASTURBATION**

Aquinas' view echoed the erotic celebration of sexual ecstasy in the **SONG OF SONGS** in the Hebrew Bible where sex is a sacred gift and picture of a mystical union, and one of the highest spiritual as well as physical forms of being.

Behold you are beautiful, my love;

behold you are beautiful;

your eyes are like doves,

Behold you are beautiful my beloved, truly lovely....

Your two breasts are like two fawns,

twins of a gazelle that feed among the lilies...

You have ravished my heart with a glance of your eyes .

(Song of Songs 1:15; 4:2, 5 & 9)

This is one of two parallel strains in the Bible – one positive and one negative, and the positive strain, that sex is to be celebrated, is echoed by Jesus himself, quoting Genesis 2:24, "from the beginning God created them male and female, and for this reason a man shall leave his mother and father and be united with his wife, and the two shall become one flesh. So what God has joined together, let no-one divide" (Mark 10:6-9). See also Paul in Ephesians 5:31.

THE NEGATIVE STRAIN

There is also a negative strain in Christianity which sees sex as dangerous, unclean, and sexual pleasure as sinful.

AUGUSTINE wrote that marriage was the "first fellowship of humankind in this mortal life", and "good not just for producing children, but also because of the natural friendship between the sexes", although primarily "a remedy for weakness, and source of comfort". Ultimately the good of marriage lay in its "goodness, fidelity and unbreakable bond".

Augustine argued against the **PELAGIANS** who saw sexual pleasure as a **NATURAL GOOD**, evil only in excess. Augustine agreed with Paul that since the **FALL** the body had been subject to death, "our body weighs heavy on our soul" with its sinful desires. Augustine believed that since the fall desire had been tainted by **LUST**. So sexual pleasure in marriage needed to be moderated by reason.

Sexual desire ("the carnal appetite") outside marriage, and sexual activity that results, "is not good , but an evil that comes from original sin". This evil of carnal lust can invade even marriage – so it is **DANGEROUS** and needs to be treated wisely and carefully.

After the **FALL** (Genesis 3) men and women were "naked and ashamed". The man's member is "no longer obedient to a quiet and normal will". Humankind was in danger of running away with lust for each other.

CONCLUSION: Augustine argues that precisely because the body is created good, it can be used wrongly, and this goodness has been deeply stained by the Fall. Sexual desire has to be circumscribed by **MODESTY**, chastity and wisdom.

CATHOLIC TEACHING TODAY

The Roman Catholic Church teaches that sex has two functions – procreative and **UNITIVE** (binding two people together). Procreation is primary. According to Humanae Vitae (1967) these two elements are **INSEPARABLE**.

> *"Sexuality becomes fully human when it is integrated into the relationship of one person to the other in lifelong gift of a man to a woman".* Catechism 2338

CHASTITY is the virtue of self-mastery (Catechism 2339). It is expressed in friendship towards our neighbour. Sex outside marriage is "gravely contrary to the dignity of persons and of human sexuality which is naturally ordered to the procreation of children". Catechism 2354

HOMOSEXUAL ACTS are "intrinsically disordered". "They are contrary to the natural law. They close the sexual act to the gift of life. Under no circumstances can they be approved". Catechism 2358

ADULTERY is absolutely forbidden by the sixth commandment and Jesus' words.

CONTRACEPTION - in 1951 Pope Pius XII officially permitted the rhythm method, but otherwise **HUMANAE VITAE** (1967) upholds the view that anything that breaks the natural relationship between sex and conception is wrong.

EVALUATION OF THE CATHOLIC VIEW

Professor Peter Gomes of Harvard University argues that the Bible bans one **CULTURAL** expression of homosexuality – a promiscuous one and "never contemplated a form of homosexuality in which loving and faithful persons sought to live out the implications of the gospel with as much fidelity as any heterosexual believer". The Good Book (1997)

The Catholic interpretation of **NATURAL LAW** implies that the primary function of sex is reproduction. But suppose the primary purpose is **BONDING**, then the argument that sex is purely for reproduction falls down – we can be Natural Law theorists and disagree about the secondary precepts (which Aquinas always argues are relative).

The Catholic **ASSUMPTION** (following Aquinas) is of one human nature. But psychology suggests there are varieties of human nature (heterosexual, homosexual, bisexual) because of genes or environment.

The prohibition on **CONTRACEPTION** seems irrational in a world of overpopulation and **STD**s. If **PRESERVATION OF LIFE** conflicts with **REPRODUCTION**, surely preservation of life is the primary **PRIMARY PRECEPT**?

SITUATION ETHICS – CHRISTIAN RELATIVISM

Joseph Fletcher sees his own theory as **RELATIVISTIC** (even though it retains one absolute principle, agape love) because any decision is made relative to circumstances.

ABSOLUTE rules must be rejected as authoritarian and unloving.

Biblical prescriptions should be followed as wise **ADVICE** but abandoned in extreme situations if love demands it.

Fletcher argues that many applications of morality are never discussed in the Bible: "Jesus said nothing about birth control, homosexuality, pre-marital intercourse , homosexuality, sex play, petting or courtship". (Fletcher, page 80).

> "It seems impossible to see any sound reason for any of the attempts to legislate morality. It is doubtful whether love's cause is helped by any of the sex laws that try to dictate sexual practices for consenting adults". Fletcher, Situation Ethics, page 80

AGAPE love (unconditional love) is the only norm. The situationist is not a 'what asker', ("what sexual practice is allowed?) but a 'who asker'. It's about **PERSONALISM** – people come first.

EVALUATION OF CHRISTIAN RELATIVISM

AGAPE is too high a standard for our personal relationships, usually governed by self-interest. Why should I be loving (rather than pleasure-seeking)?

The vulnerable (young, homeless, poor) need the protection of laws preventing **ABUSE** and **EXPLOITATION**.

We cannot predict **CONSEQUENCES** eg unwanted pregnancies or **STD**s happen to people not expecting them who may honestly believe they love the other person.

HOMOSEXUAL ACTS – A TEST CASE

We have already seen that the Catholic Church condemns homosexual behaviour as intrinsically disordered because of the assumption of one **UNIFORM HUMAN NATURE**. The situationist takes the opposite view; such legalism is unloving and so wrong. Is there a middle way?

In the **ANGLICAN** church there are two gay bishops (in America) and many practising gay priests. **VIRTUE ETHICS** indicates there is a third way of analysing homosexual behaviour. Which **VIRTUES** are present in the relationship? The **EXCESS** of promiscuity is condemned, but faithfulness, care and compassion can apply in any relationship irrespective of orientation. By the same argument the **DEFICIENCY** of abstinence is also a character **VICE**.

The moral issue surrounding homosexuality should therefore be about the promiscuous lifestyle and irresponsible spread of disease (as with heterosexuals). The legalism of natural law or over-emphasis on the code of Leviticus blinds us to the true moral question. What **VALUES** do we need in order to **FLOURISH**?

KANT on SEX

Kant asks us to commit to build the moral world – the **SUMMUM BONUM** or greatest good, by following the rational principle he calls the **CATEGORICAL IMPERATIVE**. This principle has to be applied in all similar circumstances without conditions – it is **ABSOLUTE**. We have to act in such a way that we can imagine a universal law where everyone follows the rule that is generated.

Humans have intrinsic **VALUE** as "ends in themselves". We must be given equal dignity and respect as autonomous rational beings.

We share an irrational nature of passions and instincts with **ANIMALS** but we can rise above these and order our lives by reason. Human sex will be different from animal urges.

LUST disturbs reason. By desiring someone simply as an object of pleasure (rather than seeing them as a whole person, with dignity and reason) we dishonour them and violate their special uniqueness as a free person. We sink to the level of animals.

> *"Sex exposes mankind to the danger of equality with the beasts...by virtue of the nature of sexual desire a person who sexually desires another person objectifies that person..and makes of the loved person an object of appetite. As soon as that*

appetite is satisfied one casts aside the person as one casts aside a lemon that has been sucked dry". Kant, Lectures on Ethics

MARRIAGE is the best expression of our sexuality. The pleasure of sex is acceptable (ie not animal) because two people surrender their dignity to each other and permit each other's bodies to be used for this purpose – it is a mutual **CONSENSUAL CONTRACT**. Reproduction is not the end of sex, Kant argues, but lifelong surrender to each other in a context of love and respect.

EVALUATION OF KANT

Kant appears to separate our **ANIMAL** nature from our **RATIONAL**. This dualism explains why he still sees sex as something belonging to the animal nature. But **FEELINGS** and **REASON** cannot be separated this way, many would argue.

Kantian ethics produces **ABSOLUTES** (Categoricals). So the absolute "no sex before marriage" applies here. But in the modern era such absolutes seem to deny the possibility of a **TEMPORARY** committed relationship – or even sex for fun.

It's possible to be a Kantian and accept **HOMOSEXUAL MARRIAGE** but not **ADULTERY**.

UTILITARIANISM

What do the utilitarians say about our four issues: contraception, pre-marital sex, adultery and homosexuality? Here we contrast two utilitarians: **MILL** (1806-73) and **SINGER** (1946-).

Mill is a **MULTILEVEL** utilitarian who follows a more **ARISTOTELEAN** idea of happiness – **EUDAIMONIA** or personal and social flourishing. He argues that we need **RULES** to protect justice and **RIGHTS**, which are the cumulative wisdom of society. But when happiness demands it, or a **CONFLICT** of values occurs, we revert to being an **ACT** utilitarian – hence multilevel (Act and Rule) utilitarianism.

Mill agreed that **CONTRACEPTION** was moral as it increased personal and social happiness, through family planning and restrictions on population growth. Today the British Humanist association writes "if contraception results in every child being a wanted child and in better, healthier lives for women, it must be a good thing". Mill was imprisoned in 1832 for distributing "diabolical handbills" advocating contraception.

Mill had found a murdered baby in a park. The practice of exposing unwanted children was widespread. Hospitals for **FOUNDLINGS** such as **CORAM** set up in Bristol in 1741, did little except institutionalise **INFANTICIDE** (child killing). Between 1728 and 1757 33% of babies born in foundling hospitals and workhouses died or were killed.

On **HOMOSEXUAL** rights Mill follows Bentham in arguing for "utilitarian equality" by which everyone's happiness counts equally. Bentham was the first philosopher to suggest legalised **SODOMY** in an unpublished paper in 1802. Freedom was a key to personal flourishing, and as long as no harm was done to any but consenting adults, (Mill's **HARM PRINCIPLE** in On Liberty) it is a private matter how people order their sex lives.

In his essay on **LIBERTY** (1859) Mill argues for **SOCIAL RIGHTS** so we can undertake "experiments in living" that give us protection from the prejudices of popular culture and "the tyranny of prevailing opinion and feeling". Mill would have approved of **COHABITATION** and pre-marital sex.

EVALUATION OF MILL

Mill was a father of the liberalism we take for granted where difference is tolerated. His brand of utilitarianism balances social justice and individual freedom and pursuit of happiness.

Utilitarianism works well looking **BACKWARDS**. The Abortion Act (1967), the Homosexual Reform Act (1967) and the Divorce Reform Act (1969) are all examples of utilitarian legislation.

Utilitarian ethics works less well looking forwards. We cannot predict **CONSEQUENCES**. So the **AIDS** epidemic can be seen as a product partly of personal freedom to adopt a promiscuous "unsafe" lifestyle. It is hard to see how a utilitarian can prevent this or even argue it is wrong if freely chosen.

Many of the greatest **SOCIAL** reforms have not been inspired by Christian values, Natural Law or Kantian ethics, but by **UTILITARIAN** considerations of social **WELFARE**. Today relatively few Christian churches accept the complete equality of women.

PREFERENCE UTILITARIANISM

Peter Singer defends the utilitarian line advanced by Mill and argued that with **HOMOSEXUALITY** "If a form of sexual activity brings satisfaction to those who take part in it, and harms no-one, what can be immoral about it?"

On **ADULTERY** preference utilitarians approve of any sexual activity which maximises the preferences of individuals, taking account the preferences of all those affected. So incest, bestiality, or adultery would all be acceptable.

Singer as argues for **CONTRACEPTION** as population growth is one of the most pressing utilitarian issues, we should "help governments make contraception and sterilisation as widespread as possible" (Practical Ethics, page 183). But overseas aid should be made conditional on adoption of contraceptives.

KEY CONFUSIONS

- "Sexual ethics is merely up to individual choice". It is a common misunderstanding of ethics that it is purely about personal choice. Yet **MILL** points out, following **ARISTOTLE**, that ethics always has a personal and a social dimension. Laws both reflect social morality and also help to mould it. So when the law was changed on homosexuality, contraception and child protection it both reflected a change in social attitudes (things once thought acceptable are now seen to be abusive and other things once criminalised are now morally accepted) and helped to form those attitudes. And if I choose to be promiscuous that affects every person I am promiscuous with.

- "Sexual behaviour is natural and doesn't do anyone any harm". This is a misunderstanding of what 'natural' means in ethics. For example, the word 'natural" in **NATURAL LAW** means 'in line with our rational natural purpose'. Certain goals are unique to human beings - for example **WORSHIP OF GOD** and even those shared with animals (**REPRODUCTION**) function in a different way to animals - we are **MORAL** beings capable of evaluating consequences, for example, and capable of understanding our social responsibility to build an orderly and co-operative society.

- "There is one heterosexual human nature". This is an **ASSUMPTION** of natural law theory which appears highly questionable. It seems there really is a **HOMOSEXUAL** human nature and also a **TRANSGENDER** human nature. The whole ethics of sexual behaviour has altered radically in the light of empirical research (such as the **KINSEY** report) and also the insights of psychologists such as **FREUD** and **JUNG**. Moreover the criticisms of a type of religious thought that equates sex with **SIN** may well still hang over in the **GUILT** that attends certain expressions of sexual behaviour. Of course, which expression is part of our ongoing ethical debate.

FUTURE QUESTIONS

1. "Religion is irrelevant in deciding issues surrounding sexual behaviour". Discuss

2. Critically evaluate the view that the ethics of sexual behaviour should be entirely private and personal.

3. "Because sexual conduct affects others, it should be subject to legislation". Discuss

4. "Normative theories are useful in what they might say about sexual ethics". Discuss

KEY QUOTES - SEXUAL ETHICS

1. *"The only purpose for which power can be rightfully exercised over any member of a civilised community against his will, is to prevent harm to others. His own good, either physical or moral, is not sufficient warrant". JS Mill*

2. *"If a form of sexual activity brings satisfaction to those who take part in it, and harms no-one, what can be immoral about it?" Peter Singer*

3. *"The pleasure derived from the union between the sexes is a pleasure: therefore, leaving aside the evils, which derive from that source here is why the legislator must do whatever is in his power so that the quantity in society is as high as possible". Jeremy Bentham*

4. *"Sex exposes mankind to the danger of equality with the beasts...by virtue of the nature of sexual desire a person who sexually desires another person objectifies that person..and makes of the loved person an object of appetite. As soon as that appetite is satisfied one casts aside the person as one casts aside a lemon that has been sucked dry ". Kant*

5. *"It seems impossible to see any sound reason for any of the attempts to legislate morality. It is doubtful whether love's cause is helped by any of the sex laws that try to dictate sexual practices for consenting adults". Joseph Fletcher*

Suggested Reading

Aquinas On Marriage Summa Theologica II-II Q153 a. 2c, a. 3c, q. 154 a. 1c, a. 2 ad 2, a. 11. (Extract available on Peped's sexualethicsteachingresources.co.uk website)

Pope Paul VI (1968) Humanae Vitae (Available on Peped's sexualethicsteachingresources.co.uk website)

Church of England House of Bishops (1991) Issues in Human Sexuality, London: Church House Publishing

Mill, J.S. (1859) On Liberty, Chapter 1

Exam Rescue Remedy

1. Build your own scaffolding which represents the logic of the theory. Use a mind map or a summary sheet.

2. Do an analysis of past questions by theme as well as by year (see philosophicalinvestigations.co.uk website for examples). Try writing your own Philosophy of Religion paper based on what hasn't come up recently.

3. Examine examiners' reports (go to their website) for clues as to how to answer a question well.

4. Use the **AREA** approach suggested in this revision guide. **ARGUMENT**- Have I explained the argument (from Plato or Kant for example)? **RESPONSE** - Have I outlined and explained a good range of responses to the argument? **EVALUATION** - Now I have clearly set out positions, what do I think of these? Is mine **A PHILOSOPHICAL** argument and why. Does the original argument stand or fall against the criticisms raised? Why or why not?

5. List relevant technical vocabulary for inclusion in essay (eg efficient cause, form of the good, analytic, synthetic).

6. Prepare key quotes from selected key authors, original/ contemporary (eg quotes list from the A level website philosophicalinvestigations.co.uk – even better, produce your own). Learn some.

7. Contrast and then evaluate different views/theories/authors as some questions ask "which approach is best?" So contrast every approach with one other and decide beforehand what you think.

8. Practise writing for 35 minutes. Don't use a computer, unless you do so in the exam.

9. Always answer and discuss the exact question in front of you, never learn a "model answer". Use your own examples (newspapers, films, documentaries, real life). Be prepared to think creatively and adapt your knowledge to the question.

10. Conclude with your view, justify it (give reasons) especially with "discuss".

Free Sample Chapters of How to Write Philosophical Essays for Religious Studies A level

New Edition completely revised

Understanding the Purpose

In this book I will concentrate on two approaches to writing philosophy essays. By 'philosophy' I mean everything included in the Religious Studies A level syllabus descriptions of ethics, philosophy and developments in religious thought, at A2 level. AS level requires a slightly different skill, as I will explain.

Let's be clear: the part a/part b distinction that exists at AS level, where you explain in part a and evaluate in part b, is not very helpful for developing essay-writing skills, because it pulls apart two skills that should be placed together (analysis and evaluation). It encourages you to learn to do something which you then unlearn at A2. For this reason OCR board has abandoned the part a/b split in its 2016 specification. Here I only consider A2 questions and answers that form one complete essay.

The two approaches I develop here I will call:

- Thesis-interpretation-development-explanation approach (**TIDE**)

- The asking questions about the question approach (**AQUAQ**)

I will also suggest they need to be used in different contexts. The first approach, **TIDE**, should be used when you clearly understand the issues involved with a particular question.

The second approach **AQUAQ** should be used especially when you are unsure what the issues are involved in the question.

After all, not all questions are crystal clear – some can be taken different ways, and even some in the past have been taken by students to refer to 18 different sections of the syllabus (see an example on page 18 below). None of this really matters. The only thing that matters is that you answer the question in an evaluative and analytical form of writing – and this too, I will teach you in this book.

Let me say at the start that not all teachers agree with my approach. In fact some teachers say things about essay-writing which I think are plainly wrong. Here is a list of some of the things you may have heard.

1. "Don't use 'I', the personal pronoun".

I think it is wrong to teach this because this is simply not true to how real philosophers argue. Real philosophy is about identifying, owning and then presenting a crystal clear argument about some quite complex ideas. To own the argument it is perfectly legitimate to use 'I'. Teachers who say it is wrong to do this maybe have never read articles by academic philosophers. Articles start with what is called an **ABSTRACT** and an abstract is a summary of the thesis of the article. The thesis is the essence of the argument expressed as a single statement (discussed more fully in the next chapter), for example, 'in this essay I will argue that free will is not compatible with determinism because determinism requires a certain mechanistic view of causation which excludes the possibility of an uncaused will'. I am not at this stage asking you to understand my argument. I am asking you to understand my **THESIS** – and I think you would agree, it is clear. Whether I successfully argue the case is a different matter which we will consider later.

2. "Don't ask questions in your essay".

This too is plainly wrong. Indeed my second approach involves interrogating the question. Imagine we face an exam question:

"Conscience is the voice of God, Discuss." What is meant by conscience? How do different thinkers such as Newman, Butler, Aquinas define it? Is the 'voice of God' a written text or something in my head? How can I know if it's really God's voice? These and other questions come to mind. Even if you don't like the idea of writing questions in your answer, at least do the interrogating as you think through your thesis.

3. "Do a general introduction of the major issues".

This is very dangerous if you're trying to be a philosopher. So many students drop grades by answering a question such as 'Explain and evaluate rule utilitarianism' by beginning with: "Mill was influenced by Bentham who was a hedonistic act utilitarian, but both come form a broader tradition which began with Epicurus and was developed by writers such as Hume as part of the general Enlightenment project to advance human welfare". This may be interesting (often it's not at all), it may be correct, but it is a big mistake because you have said nothing about rule utilitarianism whatever. You have wasted time and given the impression that you are a 'throw everything at the question and hope' sort of candidate, destined to achieve no greater than a C grade.

As the book progresses we will look at specific examples and explain what is good and bad about them. You can always do the same with an unmarked essay, in groups, trying to identify the kind of mistakes which I will summarise at the end of this book, together with a list of good things to aim for.

Here is a summary of a general strategy or purpose which we can practise and adopt as away of ensuring an A grade.

1. Attack the question

Questions contain ambiguous words, but they cannot contain any technical words not in the specification. A word like 'faith' which might appear in a question on the new Developments in Christian Thought OCR paper, is in fact highly ambiguous. It can mean "belief about" as in "I believe in the credal statements of the Church". It can mean 'optimism about the future' as in 'I have faith he will turn up tomorrow". And it can mean 'trust' as in "I have faith in Jesus Christ - he will get me through this mess".

Such ambiguity is found in the definitions of faith themselves, so we need to be careful not just to state a definition and leave it there (hanging in the air), but to discuss it fully. Just because someone learned has come up with a definition, doesn't mean the definition isn't itself in need of explanation and evaluation - it may be a very one-sided or deficient definition which you don't want to integrate into your argument. So leave it out, or integrate it properly.

For example, consider the Bible's own definition of faith found in the book of Hebrews (the author is unknown).

"Faith is confidence in what we hope for and assurance about what we do not see." Hebrews 11.1

This definition is future-orientated - it speaks of faith which is directed towards future events. In this sense it cannot be talking about faith in historical events such as the life of Jesus. It must be speaking **ESCHATOLOGICALLY** perhaps about events at the end times (eschaton) when Christians believe the world will be wound up in one great second coming of Christ and a judgement. In Matthew's gospel we read of how at the end of time the 'sheep will be separated from the goats' according to how we have treated 'the least of all these" (Matthew 25).

Then the writer goes on to speak of 'things we do not see' such as the presence of God and the work of the Holy Spirit. God is invisible. He is also, many have faith to believe, immortal, omnipotent, holy, and magnificent. Perhaps the writer is referring to Christian belief in the great mystery of the Godhead, Father, Son and Holy Spirit, and their characteristics.

But (to make an evaluative point) what is missing from the definition in Hebrews? It says nothing about historical facts (which also may need faith to believe) such as the supposed 'fact' of the resurrection of Jesus. It says nothing, moreover, about personal relationship. Perhaps personal relationship is the key because it involves trust. Christians believe in a person who is present by the spirit and with whom it is meaningful to say 'I have a relationship with Christ". Now we are moving faith onto different territory - it is up to us in writing the essay to say which territory we wish to march across in our answer.

2. Answer the question

It sounds almost ridiculous when we say this: the greatest mistake students make every year at A level is not to answer the question in front of them. Instead, they answer a different question, and a model answer they have in their head is then supplied which occasionally they try to twist round to this question. Let me say now: this is a disastrous tactic if you want to get an A grade.

The corollary of this is that the same question can be asked in lots of different ways and we need to learn to spot them. For example, imagine we have a question on meta-ethics (that is, on the meaning of moral language) which says:

"Moral language is just the expression of feelings". Discuss.

This was the view of the emotivist philosopher AJ Ayer. But we can ask the same question a number of different ways.

"Emotivism is a valid theory of ethical language". Discuss

Or even what appears to be the opposite statement could be seen to be a reworking of this same answer:

"Moral language is based on facts, not feelings", Discuss.

This brings me to my third purpose in launching the essay.

3. Discuss the question even if it doesn't have the word 'discuss' in it

Later we will introduce and consider the place of 'trigger words' which are words which define what the examiner is asking you to do. "Discuss' is itself a trigger word. But what about this trigger, the phrase 'to what extent'?

"TO WHAT EXTENT is the ontological argument a valid argument for God's existence?"

The meaning of the 'to what extent' itself needs to be discussed. The question is asking whether there is validity in the ontological argument in its assumptions (some times called its preconditions), which include the view that the definition of God is ;'that which no greater thing can be conceived". Is this a 'good' definition of God and a valid starting point? Is it reasonable to have **A PRIORI** starting points for God's existence, or is God always going to be an argument about experience and fact - how things are and what we find by experience of actually living? The a priori is essentially an abstraction, meaning 'before experience'. But is the abstraction itself valid?

Then there is the question of how the ontological argument proceeds. It is essentially what is called a syllogism or logical relation between a number of statements.

a. God is greater than anything that can be conceived.

b. Because non-existence is an imperfection of being - a more perfect idea of being exists which must include existence.

c. Therefore God, who has no imperfections, must exist.

As Gaunilo pointed out at the time, I can imagine a perfect island - an island greater than which cannot be conceived, but this doesn't imply the island actually exists. There is a false leap of logic included in the argument.

So our argument might be: "the ontological argument is invalid both in its preconditions, its process of reasoning, and in its conclusion. It is valid in no sense of the three implied meanings of the word 'valid' and so, to conclude, it is valid to no extent".

4. Take the question as you want to take it

In June 2015 the following question was asked in the OCR exam.

"Evaluate the claim that moral judgements are based on an unquestionable intuitive knowledge of what is good". *(OCR, 2015)*

Candidates split 50/50 as to whether this was a meta-ethics question (on the meaning of the word 'good') or whether it was a question about the meaning and role of conscience - as one definition of conscience, Aquinas' **SYNDERESIS**, means just this - an intuitive knowledge and inclination towards the good as an innate, shared state of human being.

Teachers rang me up describing how students had came out of the exam in tears because they believed the other interpretation of the question to the one they took was correct. But if they understood philosophy properly they would have grasped that any interpretation is valid depending how you argue your case. So have the courage to take the question as you want to take it.

Just to underline this point: this is what the examiner wrote in the mark scheme on this question:

Either a meta-ethical or a conscience approach to this question could be credited. Candidates could also use a combination of meta-ethics and conscience to answer this question.

Alternatively, some candidates may make the link that 'good' is known through practical decision making. They may include utilitarian concepts of hedonic naturalism where good is known by what gives pleasure, or might suggest a virtue ethics approach as a way of overcoming Moore's mysterious 'good' and the naturalistic fallacy with the point that there is not a fact/value problem with this approach and that Moore was part of the problem described by Anscombe.

Candidates may wish to define what they mean by 'moral judgements' (OCR Mark Scheme, G582 Q2, June 2015)

I think the examiner here is referring to Anscombe's 1956 essay which argues that moral philosophy has argued itself into a dead end and lost its way with the obsession with the meaning of the word 'good', and the neglect of the role of character in ethics. I'm not sure if any candidates followed the third route suggested by the examiner - which would have taken some nerve, in arguing that 'goodness' emerges through practical decision-making by an experiential route.

The Night Before the Exam

I have assumed throughout his book that you are an exam candidate, and so I want to write a chapter for you to read the night before the exam, which distills the advice we have been trying to demonstrate here.

Essentially there are two methods of writing essays on Philosophy, Ethics and Christian Thought.

METHOD 1: The thesis approach **TIDE**

In this approach, discussed in the second chapter, we state our thesis (conclusion) early in the first paragraph. We then develop the thesis in the body of the essay, illustrating it briefly and intelligently and presenting contrasting views if we so wish, (which we reject with good reasons). The thesis is then restated in a slightly fuller way (to reflect the careful analysis that precedes it) as a conclusion. **We should use this method when we are confident we understand the question and its implications**.

METHOD 2: The 'ask questions about the question' approach **AQUAQ**

Quite often we may not be very confident about what the question is driving at. If this is the case, then we must adopt the tactic of interrogating the question or asking questions about the question. I suggest we ask three questions and then spend a paragraph answering each one before coming to a conclusion. Each question focuses on one element of the exam question. **We should use this method when we are not fully confident about what the question involves.**

An example might help here. Suppose I have a question on ethics which asks:

"The ethical issues around abortion cannot be resolved without first resolving the issue of personhood".

What are the ethical issues surrounding abortion? How and with what ethical tools are these issues resolved? What is meant by the concept of personhood? These three questions (none of which have a single answer), woven into an opening paragraph, give the answer a clear, relevant structure - and the thesis should emerge as we develop our essay. The conclusion is then presented as our own answer to these three questions, perhaps arrived at by contrasting the views of specific philosophers and setting up two ethical theories to see how the idea of personhood is relevant to each.

An equivalent example in Philosophy might address the title "Religious Language is meaningless.", Discuss. The questions you might ask in your opening paragraph might include: What do we mean by religious language? Are there different rules for religious language when compared to everyday language? How is the word 'meaning' to be understood?

When you arrive in the exam room, you must follow the steps set out below.

Read every question and highlight key words

Every year candidates make the fundamental error of learning a previous essay off by heart and then regurgitating it in the exam. And every year the examiner complains that candidates did not answer the question. So take a highlighter pen in with you and

1. Highlight all the **trigger/command** words (words like "explain", "to what extent", "discuss"). And then

2. Highlight any words that are **unusual** or unexpected.

If the trigger word is **explain** it is not asking us to **evaluate.** For example "explain the main principles of classical utilitarianism" has the unusual word "classical" in there. By focusing on this word and highlighting it, you are forced to ask the question "what is classical utilitarianism?" and so there is at least a chance that you will avoid the irrelevance of talking about Peter Singer, who is a modern utilitarian.

For Philosophy, sometimes a very specific question is asked to highlight an aspect of an argument, for example, 'Explain Descartes' ontological argument for the existence of God'. It won't gain marks if you go through other ontological arguments as this is not what the question is asking (you could highlight one or two differences, but only to stress the points that Descartes is making). Remember that when a scholar is mentioned in the syllabus, the question can be entirely addressed to that scholar - so the night before go through the syllabus check which scholars might come up.

But (just to be absolutely clear about this) at **A2 level** we are expected to interweave analysis and evaluation, and this is made clear by trigger words such as "discuss", "assess" or "to what extent".

Sketch out your thesis/ key questions about the question

Always make sure there is some additional loose paper on your desk (put your hand up before the exam starts and request it). Then sketch out quickly your thesis, the main points you need to develop it, and any illustrations you may use. If you are genuinely unsure about the question, don't worry: every other candidate is probably unsure as well. Then use method 2 and ask three questions about the question and impose your own interpretation on it. You will gain credit by this considered and well-directed line which will then emerge as your answer.

My strong advice would be to practise sequencing ideas before the exam, and to have you own mind-map prepared and memorised which you can quickly sketch on a piece of paper as a memory aid.

Be bold in your answer

It's surprising how many candidates come up with statements such as "there are many arguments for and against the ontological argument, and the issue remains difficult to resolve". This is a form of intellectual cowardice which gains no marks at all. Be bold in what you argue, and try hard to justify your approach with good, solid reasons. It is the quality of the argument which gains credit in philosophical writing, not the conclusion you arrive at. Of course, it essential that the conclusion follows.

Analyse, don't just assert

It is tempting to throw down everything you know about, say, utilitarianism in a series of unconnected assertions.

> *"Utilitarianism is teleological, consequentialist and relativistic. It sets up the Greatest Happiness Principle. Utilitarians also believe the end justifies the means."*

These are just assertions which are peppered liberally with what we call technical language (that is language no-one in the real world ever uses). Notice that the above opening few lines demonstrate no understanding and no analytical ability. Instead we should be aiming to write more like this:

> *"Utilitarianism is a theory of rational desire which holds to one intrinsic good: pleasure or happiness. By the greatest happiness principle utilitarians seek to maximise this good in two ways: they seek to maximise net happiness (happiness minus misery) for the maximum number of people. So it is an aggregating theory, where goodness is added up from individual desires to produce an overall maximum good in which "everyone counts as one" (Bentham)."*

You should avoid phrases like 'this famous philosopher' and 'this issue has been debated for centuries'. Is this true? How would we know? Avoid these kinds of broad, sweeping generalisations.

Illustrate your argument

I remember reading an exam report at University which mentioned that one candidate had been highly commended in an essay on utilitarianism for discussing the case of Captain Oates who, during Scott's doomed Antarctic expedition in 1912, walked out of the storm-bound tent in order to sacrifice himself to save his friends, with the words "I may be gone some considerable time". It's an interesting example because it suggests that a utilitarian could be capable of heroic sacrifice rather than the usual illustration candidates give of torturing a terror suspect to find a bomb location.

Spend a few moments working out which examples you will discuss to illustrate key theories and their application. You can pre-prepare them especially in Ethics, and in Philosophy of Religion you can pre-prepare the contrasting arguments which philosophers bring to many of the syllabus areas.

In Philosophy of Religion this advice applies especially to areas such as religious language and the analogies told by Flew (Wisdom's gardener), Hare (three blik illustrations) and Mitchell, (The Stranger), though be concise in how you illustrate these examples - always make them serve the point you are making and not the other way round.

What is the examiner looking for?

In summary the examiner is looking for three things:

Relevance - every sentence linked to the question set and to your main thesis.

Coherence - every sentence and paragraph should "hang together' or cohere. The linkages should be clear as the analysis proceeds.

Clarity - your style should be clear, and in the context, the philosophical vocabulary you use should be clear. You don't necessarily have to define every technical word, but if it does need a little clarification, you can always use brackets for economy. For example:

"Utilitarianism is a teleological (end-focused) theory combining an idea of intrinsic goodness with a method of assessing that goodness by considering consequences".

An example in philosophy would be:

"The Falsification Principle argues that for any statement to be treated as a proposition it must deny at least one state of affairs rather than affirm all outcomes by expanding its criteria, (and in doing so, 'dying the death of a thousand qualifications', as Flew notes)."

Postscript

Peter Baron read Politics, Philosophy and Economics at New College, Oxford and afterwards obtained an MLitt for a research degree in Hermeneutics at Newcastle University. He qualified as an Economics teacher in 1982, and taught ethics at Wells Cathedral School in Somerset from 2006-2012. He is currently a freelance writer and speaker.

In 2007 he set up a philosophy and ethics community dedicated to enlarging the teaching of philosophy in schools by applying the theory of multiple intelligences to the analysis of philosophical and ethical problems. So far over 700 schools have joined the community and over 30,000 individuals use his website every month.

To join the community please register your interest by filling in your details on the form on the website. We welcome contributions and suggestions so that our community continues to flourish and expand.

www.peped.org contains **EXTRACTS** and **FURTHER READING** mentioned in the exam specification, plus additional articles, handouts and essay plans. Notice that the exam specification merely gives guidance as to further reading - you may use any source or philosopher you find relevant to the construction of your argument. Indeed, if you have the courage to abandon the selection (and any examples) introduced by your textbook, you will relieve the examiner of boredom and arguably launch yourself on an A grade trajectory.

23642791R00063

Printed in Poland
by Amazon Fulfillment
Poland Sp. z o.o., Wrocław